FREE
YOURSELF
FROM
ANXIETY

At **www.howto.co.uk** you can engage in conversation with our authors – all of whom have 'been there and done that' in their specialist fields. You can get access to special offers and additional content but most importantly you will be able to engage with, and become a part of, a wide and growing community of people just like yourself.

At **www.howto.co.uk** you'll be able to talk and share tips with people who have similar interests and are facing similar challenges in their life. People who, just like you, have the desire to change their lives for the better – be it through moving to a new country, starting a new business, growing your own vegetables, or writing a novel.

At **www.howto.co.uk** you'll find the support and encouragement you need to help make your aspirations a reality.

For more information on anxiety and the opportunity to engage with the authors of this book, Emma Fletcher and Martha Langley, visit www.freeyourselffromanxiety.co.uk.

How To Books strives to present authentic, inspiring, practical information in their books. Now, when you buy a title from **How To Books**, you get even more than words on a page.

FREE YOURSELF FROM ANXIETY

A self-help guide to overcoming anxiety disorders

EMMA FLETCHER
AND
MARTHA LANGLEY

howtobooks

Published by How To Books Ltd,
Spring Hill House, Spring Hill Road,
Begbroke, Oxford OX5 1RX, United Kingdom
Tel: (01865) 375794. Fax: (01865) 379162.
info@howtobooks.co.uk
www.howtobooks.co.uk

How To Books greatly reduce the carbon footprint of their books by sourcing their typesetting and printing in the UK.

British Library Cataloguing in Publication Data
A catalogue record for this book is available from the British Library

ISBN 978 1 84528 311 7

First edition 2009

Cover design by Baseline Arts Ltd, Oxford
Produced for How To Books by Deer Park Productions, Tavistock, Devon
Typeset by PDQ Typesetting, Newcastle-under-Lyme, Staffs.
Printed and bound by Bell & Bain Ltd, Glasgow

NOTE: The material contained in this book is set out in good faith for general guidance and no liability can be accepted for loss or expense incurred as a result of relying in particular circumstances on statements made in the book. Laws and regulations are complex and liable to change, and readers should check the current position with the relevant authorities before making personal arrangements.

Contents

Who this book is for

This book is intended for people affected by all forms of Anxiety: phobias (including agoraphobia and social phobia), obsessive compulsive disorder, panic attacks and generalised anxiety disorder. We do not recommend using this book if you suffer from post-traumatic stress disorder or for anxiety problems in young people and children.

Acknowledgements

Emma and Martha would like to thank: The Group, for the time they gave to this project; Angela, Chris and Isabelle for their feedback on the text; First Steps to Freedom, and No Panic.

Dedication

Emma and Martha dedicate this book to all the volunteers who give their time to helping people with Anxiety.

1 The Black Hole of Anxiety

The black hole of anxiety

For most people, anxiety seems to come from nowhere and hit them like a sledgehammer. One minute, more or less happily living your life, the next, terrified and distraught, struggling to breathe perhaps, convinced you are dying, or that someone else will die and it will all be your fault.

Maybe you visit your doctor straight away, maybe you struggle on alone for as long as you can, but sooner or later you will be told that it's Anxiety. Just anxiety.

This doesn't make any sense. You know what anxiety is. It's glancing at the clock and wondering uneasily why someone is late. It's double checking that you put the handbrake on when parking on a hill. It's not this living nightmare that turns every minute of every day into a torment of worrying.

Except that it is. Your normal anxiety has got out of control and turned into an Anxiety Disorder. In other words, everybody has some anxiety, but not everybody has Anxiety. In this book, when we give anxiety a capital 'A' we are talking about an illness, and you can recover from it. There is good help available on the NHS, but it can mean a long wait as your name works its way up the list. If you are housebound, the wait for a visiting therapist is likely to be even longer. Why not try to help yourself in the meantime?

Some people are able to stage a full recovery through self-help. Others may still need help from a professional to finish their work, but they will go into the sessions armed with self-knowledge and an improved understanding of their illness.

Anxiety is a black hole. It sucks in your hopes, your pleasures, your plans for the future and above all your energy. It's picky though. It leaves behind fears, worries, and exhaustion. No wonder it's hard to pick yourself up and find the energy for a recovery programme. No wonder you feel like staying in your safe place and doing as little as possible.

It is possible to turn this round. It is possible to come back from the black hole of Anxiety. The aim of this book is to help you set up and follow a self-help recovery programme. Working at your own pace, in small steps, you can learn to let go of Anxiety and reclaim your life.

Getting equipped

There are two basic things that you need.

A notebook – you will need to write things down as you work through this book. A notebook is better than a collection of scraps of paper, because sometimes you'll want to look back and see how far you've progressed.

A relaxation tape or CD – organize this now, before you start work, so that you have it to hand when you need it. You can buy them in any music store, and often in health food shops and chemists. If you are housebound you could ask someone to get it for you, or use the mail order service provided by the charities in this field (see Appendix 2 for their contact details).

Deep relaxation is an important part of recovery from Anxiety. This is not the same as relaxing in front of the TV, or with a book, or anything else you may choose. These are all good for you, but you will also need to learn to do full relaxation. There is more about this in Chapter 6.

You should aim for a recording with a voice on it, rather than just music, and there are two main types:

- **Progressive muscle relaxation:** the voice talks you through the process of clenching and relaxing every muscle in your body.

- **Visualisation:** the voice describes a relaxing scene, such as a beautiful garden or a deserted tropical beach.

Choose whichever type appeals to you most. It is okay to buy one of each and decide which you prefer after playing them. If you don't like the idea of listening to a strange voice, then you can record your own voice, or ask a trusted person to record it for you. See Extra Information 1.1 for a script that you can record.

Group members talk

All of the examples in this book are taken from real life, from the stories of people with Anxiety who either told us about their experiences or wrote them down for us. We haven't changed their words. They all understand the suffering that Anxiety causes. Let's meet the group:

'I was on tranquillisers for 36 years and your body becomes tolerant and you start to feel anxiety symptoms which get worse when you stop taking them.'
ANDREA

'I had an older brother who was cleverer than me, and I developed a stammer when I was 8 years old which made me very self-conscious.'
ANDREW

'I was on the bus going to visit my mother and I started to feel floaty and scared and out-of-sorts. I thought I was going to have a heart attack. I wasn't able to breathe, I felt I was losing my breath.'
BRIDGET

'... my mother has told me I was an unsettled baby and I think I was quite an anxious child. I never felt safe, perhaps because of a traumatic experience when I was 4 years old.'
JULIE

'to my horror [I] overheard someone say that...my dad had died...I don't remember questioning my mother as to the truth...my mother seemed distant from me...unfortunately, her inability to alleviate my sorrow had a profound effect on me.'
MARGARET HAWKINS, CHAIRPERSON OF NO PANIC

'I hear people say they feel as if some power from somewhere has cursed them with this strange madness for life, and that no one else in the world has this problem.'
NORMAN

'I had two upsetting events as a young child, when an older boy exposed himself to me and I ran all the way home and then when I was 6, I had my tonsils out in hospital. They gave you a ride on a rocking horse and when you turned round your mum had gone...just like that! In those days parents weren't allowed to visit, a whole week with no contact!'
PEN

'I had a traumatic experience when I was about 13 – I was raped... Now, I have flashbacks, like a video in my head. Feel anxious all the time. I am still extremely scared to go to places associated with where it happened.'
SARAH

'School was terrifying, I was so self-conscious. I took a lot of time off. I thought I was weird, not normal.'
TERESA

'My first experience of anxiety was when I was 13, in the 1950s. I was going into school assembly and I just wanted to come out, I felt I'd pass out any minute. I was very hot and we were stood there for 20 minutes or more.'
WENDY

We are very grateful to them all for being willing to share their stories. You will learn that they're in various stages of recovery. Several of them are volunteers with charities such as No Panic and First Steps to Freedom. The full version of Margaret's story is available from No Panic, see Appendix 2 for contact details.

Ways of using this book

You may feel ready to undertake the challenge of working towards a full recovery. You may feel interested in the idea, but nervous about it. Or you may feel a deep resistance to it. Whatever your current feeling is about recovery, whether you feel optimistic, pessimistic or somewhere in between, you can use this book to make a start.

You can use the ideas and exercises in whatever way suits you best at the present time, and you can come back to them at a later date when you are ready for more progress. There are four particular ways in which this book can help:

1. **Relief from the worst aspects of Anxiety and managing your present life better.**
    You'll acquire a set of simple tools that will help you to feel better, more in control of your life and more confident. By learning to relax, taking more exercise, eating and drinking more sensibly, learning not to fear panic attacks, practising self-exposure and turning negative thoughts to positive, you'll feel more able to cope with your life as it is now.

2. **Recovering from your current bout of Anxiety**
    There are a lot of different techniques explained in this book. As you work through them you'll build a complete portfolio for Anxiety management. Not all of them will work for everybody, but the only way to find out is to try each one. You'll then be able to create your own individual recovery programme.

3. **Dealing with problems in the future**

   Even when you are over the worst, setbacks can occur. Life will continue to present challenges. If you are prepared for them, they won't overwhelm you or send you hurrying back to your safe retreat. Once you have worked through this book you will have the skills you need to prevent relapses. You'll be able to recognise the early warning signs of Anxiety, and you'll know which techniques work best for you so that you deal with it before it takes hold. And if you do experience a setback, you can review the situation and ask yourself what you can learn from it and how you could have done things differently. This is more than first aid – these are tools for life, and a life which is less Anxiety-prone.

4. **Growing as a person and developing unused potential**

   As you look deeper into the causes of your Anxiety you may feel the need to make changes in your life. You can choose how far down the road you travel. If you are satisfied with levels 1, 2 or 3 then that's fine. The important thing is that you can make your own choices about important areas in your life – this is a truly healthy state. When Anxiety rules your life, you feel trapped or bullied by it, but when you work through this book you'll start to take back control.

Exercise

In your notebook, make two lists, headed 'things I have to do' and 'things I can't do.' Include the things that Anxiety makes you do, or stops you doing, and anything else that you feel you must do or can't do. Here's a brief example:

I have to stay at home
I have to cook for the family
I can't go in the garden
I can't control my dog

Now rewrite each list. Instead of 'have to' write 'choose to'. Instead of 'can't' write 'choose not to'.

I choose to stay at home
I choose to cook for the family
I choose not to go in the garden
I choose not to control my dog

Suddenly you can see that you to have more choice than you thought. This can be a powerful turning point – and remember, it includes the choice *not* to change. If you have truly weighed up the pros and cons, the gains and losses, you may decide it's okay to settle for level one, or two, or three.

GROUP MEMBERS TALK

'I have general anxiety due to withdrawal from tranquillisers.'
ANDREA

'I have suffered from OCD most of my life.'
ANDREW

'In the end my diagnosis was panic attack.'
BRIDGET

'I've had panic, agoraphobia, death phobia, social phobia, illness phobia and claustrophobia.'
JULIE

'[I] could not shake off the feelings of dread . . . I was constantly in a state of fear.'
MARGARET

'My very first recollection of any symptoms resembling that of obsessive-compulsive disorder began to reveal themselves to me as a child.'
NORMAN

'I have agoraphobia and GAD.'
PEN

'I have Borderline Personality Disorder and chronic Post-traumatic Stress Disorder.'
SARAH

'From what I know today I reckon I had social phobia.'
TERESA

'I'm a recovering agoraphobic.'
WENDY

Part One

2 Are You Sure it's Anxiety?

A person having their first panic attack can think they're having a heart attack. Someone calls an ambulance, they are taken to Accident and Emergency, and after the usual tests they are told that it's panic. The most common reactions to this news are embarrassment and disbelief, but at least they've been seen by a doctor and can start the process of coming to terms with what has happened to them.

At the other end of the scale, some people live with their illness for years without having it properly diagnosed, without talking to anyone about it and without getting any help.

Seeing the doctor

Quite simply, everyone needs to see a doctor to discuss their symptoms and get a diagnosis. There are a few physical illnesses whose symptoms are just like Anxiety so you need to make sure that you're not suffering from one of those. There is no point in reading this book and doing the work we suggest if, for instance, you are suffering from a thyroid problem that can be treated by tablets.

So if you haven't seen your doctor yet, now is the time to do so. If you are nervous about doing this, consider taking someone sympathetic along with you for support. If you are housebound, ask for a home visit.

The important thing to remember is, that if it turns out you do have an Anxiety disorder, it is an illness and it is not your fault, so you really don't need to be embarrassed.

Sometimes people worry that their medical records will always show that they've had a problem, and this will go against them in some way. And yet these problems are extremely common, so there must be thousands of people with similar records who are now leading happy and fulfilled lives. Wouldn't you like to be one of them?

What will the doctor do?

You can expect the doctor to listen to what you have to say, and ask you a few questions. He or she will probably do a few simple checks to rule out a physical cause. If a blood test is suggested and needles are a problem for you, then say so. Even if the blood test has to wait for another visit, you will have made your first steps towards recovery.

How shall I talk to the doctor?

Sometimes people worry about how they are going to explain what they are feeling. It might help to make a list beforehand of all the sensations you experience. If you need to talk about one incident, then don't talk too much about the build-up to it. A simple statement will get the conversation started and the doctor can ask you questions to get more information.

'I was standing in the queue at the bank when I suddenly felt terribly sick, my heart started pounding and I felt like my legs wouldn't hold me.'

If you need to describe a continuous feeling, again keep it simple:

'I feel so shaky every morning that I just can't get out of bed, and I get worse as the day goes on.'

'I keep needing to check that the smoke alarm works, I know it does, but sometimes I go back 20 times to it. It can take me all morning to get past it.'

Remember these remarks are just to get you started. You may not yet feel able to ask the questions that really haunt you: Am I going mad? Will my heart stop beating? Never mind. You've made a start.

And while we're on the subject, let's answer those two questions. A person with Anxiety is not going mad, and neither Anxiety nor panic will make anyone's heart stop beating.

What will happen next?

There are various things the doctor can suggest to help you:

- **Let's wait and see:** if your Anxiety is very new, it can be a sensible idea to wait a couple of weeks to see if it subsides. If that is suggested, use the time to give yourself some TLC and to make the changes we suggest in Part One.

- **A short course of tranquillisers**: although doctors now understand that tranquillisers are addictive if used for too long, taking them for a short time can help someone over a difficult patch.

- **Other medication**: you may be asked to try beta-blockers or anti-depressants. Sometimes you may need to try more than one anti-depressant to find the right one for you.

- **Counselling:** many surgeries have a counsellor who can talk to patients. Expect to have to wait for an appointment.

- **A mental health nurse:** some practices have a Community Psychiatric Nurse (or CPN) who can work with patients.

- **Referral to a mental health unit:** your doctor may offer to refer you to a hospital consultant, but waiting lists can be very long.

Did it worry you when you saw the words 'mental health'? Anxiety is a mental health problem, but mental health is a term that covers a huge range of issues and only a few of them are long-term permanent problems.

If you are offered therapy, one of the most common approaches is called cognitive behaviour therapy. It is very successful in helping people with Anxiety and this book is based on its techniques, so you will learn more about it as you work through the book.

GROUP MEMBERS TALK ABOUT DIAGNOSIS

'I was diagnosed by my GP.'
ANDREA

'[I] was diagnosed by a doctor in my early 20s.'
ANDREW

'I was near my GP so I went there and he saw me straight away, he did a few tests and then sent me to hospital, he thought it was panic but he wanted to be sure.'
BRIDGET

'I was diagnosed by doctors, but I had a problem accepting that it was anxiety and not a physical health problem.'
JULIE

'I must have been in the surgery with my GP for at least half an hour. He proceeded to explain to me that I had developed what was then called obsessional-compulsive neurosis.'
NORMAN

'My first diagnosis was neurasthenia, the word agoraphobia was used much later. A doctor said to me "it's like there are too many packs of peas in the freezer, and the lid won't close it goes into melt down."'
PEN

'I was diagnosed at my first hospital admission, age 16. I was diagnosed with PTSD quickly but not much was done about it.'
SARAH

'The doctor diagnosed depression. I think he prescribed Librium.'
TERESA

'Our doctor was ahead of the times, he gave me some tablets but he also sent me to our vicar, who was a counsellor working at the surgery, and he gave me the diagnosis.'
WENDY

3 Depression

Many people with Anxiety also suffer from clinical depression. For some people the misery of Anxiety is the cause of their depression, but for others the depression comes first, and Anxiety is a secondary effect of the depression.

Depression is not just a case of feeling low, or of needing to cheer yourself up. Clinical depression is an illness. Here is a list of symptoms (you are unlikely to experience all of them):

- depressed mood most of the day, nearly every day
- tiredness. No energy
- feeling guilty, feeling worthless, blaming yourself
- taking no pleasure or interest in your usual activities
- problems with memory or concentration
- changes in appetite and sleeping pattern
- withdrawal from people and social activities
- restlessness
- irritability and anger
- feeling pessimistic and hopeless
- thinking about death, or contemplating suicide.

Mild depression can be treated through self-help – exercise is particularly helpful. More severe depression will need help from your doctor, in the form of anti-depressant tablets or visits to a counsellor.

Can I work on my anxiety while I have depression?

If you have depression, whatever has caused it, you will have to decide whether to work on the depression before you turn your attention to your Anxiety. The key is to examine your motivation and your energy levels. Depression saps both, and without them self-help can be very difficult.

This decision is complicated by the fact that you are bound to feel a bit daunted at the start of a self-help programme – the journey seems so long, and the ultimate goal of recovery so very unobtainable.

We suggest that you don't think at all about the ultimate goal at the moment. Just think about the next step. It will be a small step, because that's how self-help works – small, steady, well-planned steps. If you think you have the energy and motivation for this, then self-help for your Anxiety is worth trying. If you can't face even the smallest step, then turn your attention to your depression before you tackle your Anxiety.

GROUP MEMBERS TALK ABOUT TREATMENT

'I tried hypnotherapy in my teens. I've never been offered medication, but I have had cognitive behaviour therapy.'
ANDREW

'I tried medication for a short time but it wasn't for me. Homeopathy and natural remedies helped quite a lot. Finally I tried anxiety management and that helped the most.'
JULIE

'Many years of my life have been wasted simply because anxiety symptoms were not explained to me. Medication dampened them down but did not cure the problem in any way, shape or form.'
MARGARET

'The medication that my GP had initially prescribed were giving me horrible side effects, they were actually making my symptoms feel worse, not better. Within a short time I was returning to see my GP once more as I was now experiencing the constant sensation of adrenaline rushing round my body almost every second of the day.'
NORMAN

'I've tried prescribed medication, herbal remedies, homeopathy, hypnosis, CBT, counselling, relaxation, meditation, graded exposure and breathing exercises. Recently I've found yoga very helpful, specially the breathing.'
PEN

'I was admitted to hospital when I was 16 after taking an overdose. This was the first of many, in adult and adolescent units in different parts of the country, following suicide attempts and episodes of self-harm (cutting, burning, solvent abuse, periods of dehydration (self-inflicted) and also periods of starvation.) I had some CBT but I wasn't then in the right mindset to use it. I've had various treatments in different hospitals.'
SARAH

'I took an overdose. I suffered from depressive/anxiety bouts off and on through several years of my marriage (I have three children, 13, 15 and 24). I participated in a study for long-term depression, I think it was cognitive therapy, approximately 8 sessions. I was on Prozac, which appeared to help. But I started to feel that my emotions were numbed. It seemed to bring out aggressive tendencies.'
TERESA

'I was on Valium for years, and I had counselling and hypnosis. Coming off Valium, I had six weeks in hospital, although I went home at weekends, but I largely did it myself, just by leaving it longer and longer before I took the next one. I haven't had a Valium since 1984.'
WENDY

4 Anxiety Disorders

This is a brief overview so don't worry if your particular phobia or obsession isn't mentioned here. As you work through this book you will learn more about the various types of Anxiety disorder, and you will be able to apply the principles of recovery to your own situation. There are more details in Extra Information 4.

Panic attacks

A panic attack is a sudden surge of Anxiety, usually short-lived but very intense. The surge causes physical sensations that increase dramatically as the attack progresses. It is fuelled by a sudden release of adrenalin into the body.

They vary from person to person but doctors use the following list – if you experience four or more of these sensations in the space of a few seconds then you are probably having a panic attack:

- shortness of breath
- a choking sensation
- rapid or irregular heartbeat
- chest pains
- tension in muscles
- trembling or shaking
- numbness
- intense sweating
- dizziness
- nausea
- urgent need to go to the toilet.

After the attack, you are left with feelings of exhaustion, shakiness and bewilderment.

For many people, panic attacks are the foundation that their Anxiety disorder is built on. For them, life becomes a question of doing anything to avoid another panic attack. And yet other Anxiety sufferers have never experienced a panic attack, and never will.

Phobias

Phobias encompass both a fear of something specific and more generalised, but still focused, fears.

Agoraphobia and claustrophobia

These are both about a fear of being trapped and unable to get help or reach a safe place. They are really a cluster of phobias which can include open spaces, closed spaces, crowded spaces, queues, lifts, public transport, crossing bridges, the hairdresser, restaurants, theatres and cinemas.

Monophobia

This is a fear of being alone.

Social phobia

This is another cluster, connected with other people. It is more than just being shy or self-conscious and can include speaking, eating or drinking in public, using public lavatories, preparing food or drink or writing while being watched. Social phobics often worry that they will give themselves away if they blush, sweat or stammer, and the worry makes it more likely that they will.

Specific phobias

These are also known as simple phobias because they focus on just one thing. There are hundreds of these, from fear of thunderstorms to fear of injections.

Generalised anxiety disorder (GAD)

GAD is different from a phobia in that you feel excessively anxious but without a specific focus. You feel tense and unable to relax. You may feel many of the symptoms of a panic attack but without the climactic rush of panic. You may also be constantly worried about something bad happening to people you care about, and you may feel that your worrying keeps these people safe. The constant worry is very distressing and can make you feel that you're out of control and might go mad.

Feeling unreal

Some people describe a strange and scary feeling of being 'not quite there', 'unreal' or 'not in my body properly'. This is not in fact an Anxiety disorder in itself, but it is mentioned so often that it needs explaining. It happens when someone breathes in a shallow, fast way, which upsets the balance of oxygen and carbon dioxide in their system. It is frightening but not dangerous.

If you've had Anxiety for a long time, and think that you know everything it can throw at you, then it can be very frightening if these feelings of unreality suddenly develop on top of everything else you have to cope with.

Obsessive compulsive disorder (OCD)

OCD starts with obsessive thoughts, which are so upsetting that you search for a way to get rid of them. If your way is to carry out compulsive behaviours then you have OCD. Compulsions often have to be repeated many times before it feels like the thought has been cancelled out.

The obsessive thoughts are often about dirt and disease, or about harming someone, either by accident or by giving way to an impulse. Thoughts about germs may lead to compulsive hand washing or cleaning. Fear of causing harm can lead to checking gas taps, electrical connections or the car.

Other compulsions may involve hoarding (newspapers, food or just rubbish), or a preoccupation with symmetry or arranging things in a particular order.

Sometimes there is an obvious link between the compulsive behaviour and the object of the obsession – e.g. dirt and washing – but in other cases there appears to be no logical connection. For example, someone believed they had to touch every lamp post they passed to prevent something dreadful happening to a member of their family.

Sometimes the compulsions are thoughts rather than actions. Obsessive thoughts about harming someone or doing something immoral or taboo, may lead to compulsive thoughts about prayer to cancel out the obsessive thoughts.

Compulsions tend to increase over time, so that you have to do a longer ritual with more repetitions to achieve the same amount of temporary reduction in Anxiety. This is exhausting of course, and so someone with OCD can eventually get to a point where they avoid as far as possible the things that trigger their compulsions. This can mean, for instance, that someone with a cleanliness obsession actually becomes quite dirty because they can't face the enormous ritual of taking a shower or washing their hair.

If you have OCD you may well have always been a methodical, accurate and careful person. You may even have had a job that exploited these useful qualities. When you are under stress your useful qualities turn to OCD.

Understanding the difference between OCD and phobias

Sometimes it can be difficult to distinguish between OCD and a phobia. There is a sense in which most Anxiety sufferers have an obsession – if you spend all your time worrying about having a panic attack, or finding

21

a spider, or meeting someone in the street, then you are obsessed to a certain extent. And you could say that behaviours such as constantly checking a room for spiders, or crossing the road to avoid a meeting, have an element of compulsion to them.

But there is an extra dimension to OCD, which is the link between the obsessions and the compulsions. A person with OCD usually has a strong feeling that they need to carry out their compulsions or else some dreadful consequence will ensue, and almost always they also feel that they must do their compulsions in a certain way, like a ritual.

So, if you are afraid of spiders and you need to check each room for them, then you have a phobia. If you feel that letting a spider be in the room is likely to bring bad luck, or harm to yourself or your family, and if you also check the room in the same way each time, then you have OCD. Similarly, someone who is anxious about the security of their home might double check that they have locked the door, whereas someone with OCD might check repeatedly, locking and unlocking.

OCD can exist alongside other Anxiety disorders, for example social and health phobias, and also depression.

Post-traumatic stress disorder (PTSD)

This is caused by exposure to danger or abuse. It is classified as an Anxiety disorder although it relates to events that have happened in the past rather than fears about what may happen in the future. Most people who experience traumatic events such as road/rail/air accidents or incidents involving violence can expect to have at least some disturbing physical and emotional reactions associated with shock and horror. Usually these are short-lived. Support from family and friends, with possible short-term professional help is usually enough to help them through it. A very few people go on to develop PTSD, where they continue to have strong reactions over a long period, usually feeling that they are re-living the trauma and unable to resume their normal lives.

PTSD needs professional treatment so we don't recommend using this book or attempting self-help.

Children and young people

This book is intended for use by adults dealing with their own Anxiety. Where children are concerned, although they may be having problems which show many of the same features as adult Anxiety disorders, we do not recommend trying to adapt a self-help approach without getting advice.

Most children go through phases when they are frightened of particular things – these are part of their normal development and are usually outgrown. If problems do persist way beyond the expected age or cause severe disruption to the child's everyday life and forming of relationships, some professional help and guidance may be needed.

It is advisable to get a proper assessment which takes into account the child's general health, overall development and any factors within the family or environment which might be contributing.

Keeping an anxiety diary

It's time to get out your notebook and start keeping a diary. An Anxiety diary is a simple record of your anxious feelings day by day. It's important that you write down your Anxiety scores at least twice a day, but there is no need for you to try to account for every minute of the day. But don't leave it till the end of the week and then try to remember everything, because you won't remember accurately enough.

Even doing it every day you will find that you tend to record the bad times, and ignore the comparatively good times. The important thing is to learn to assess your Anxiety by scoring it. Be honest, only you will ever see the diary.

Key skill: keeping an anxiety diary

DAY	TIME	ACTIVITY	ANXIETY SCORE

Anxiety is scored out of 10, where '0' is no Anxiety at all and '10' is the worst Anxiety you can ever imagine anybody feeling. Here are some sample entries:

DAY	TIME	ACTIVITY	ANXIETY SCORE
Monday	10.30	queuing in bank	7
Monday	11.00	back home	3
Saturday	15.00	checking cooker	6
Saturday	17.00	resting	4

If you are concerned about your privacy, then use a code or whatever system you can understand.

Sometimes it helps people to write more about what they are going through. Do this if you wish – maybe in the back of the notebook.

GROUP MEMBERS TALK ABOUT THE ANXIETY EXPERIENCE

'When I was 34 my mother died suddenly when I was with her. It was a terrible event that made my anxiety much worse.'
ANDREA

'Like many OCD sufferers I have an overwhelming fear of losing control.'
ANDREW

'The Bully was ever present, turning my legs into jelly, causing my heart to race... and so on... Every sufferer will know what I mean.'
JULIE

'I checked each night to make sure that no knives were left on the work surfaces and as the thoughts became more insistent I transferred this uneasy feeling to all sharp objects.'
MARGARET

> 'It's time to rise and time to shower.
> Will all of today be controlled by its power?
> When placing my feet upon the floor
> They have to be right or it's mental war.
> Where's the soap, has it been used?
> Non sufferers would be highly amused.'

NORMAN

5 Helping Yourself to Overcome Anxiety

Dealing with most health problems involves a degree of self-help. Even something as simple as remembering to take your tablets is self-help. Someone with a joint injury may be given exercises to practise at home, a diabetic will be given dietary rules, or a heart patient will be given lifestyle advice.

In the case of Anxiety disorders, the self-help element is crucial. The best therapist in the world can't help you if you don't co-operate with them, and drugs will only dampen the symptoms down to a level where you feel able to do the work that's needed.

Every time you talk your problems through with a sympathetic friend or family member you are helping yourself. Reading around the topic will help you to understand your illness. In some areas there are self-help groups, where people meet up to socialise and offer support to each other. Finally, there are the telephone helplines, run by volunteers who are almost all sufferers themselves – see Appendix 2 for more on these.

So whatever treatment route you choose, self-help will be involved. This book, however, offers you a complete approach to self-help. You can use it entirely on your own, or in tandem with other help – but do please mention to your therapist that you are using it.

Qualities needed for self-help

Anyone can apply the principles of self-help. It doesn't matter if your Anxiety is mild or severe, new or long-standing. There is always something you can do to start yourself on the road to recovery. What personal qualities do you need?

- **Commitment**: you may be at the stage of researching your options, with the intention of leafing through this book to see what it's like. That's fine, but when you are ready to start work it's best to do so with the determination to give it a fair chance.

- **Time**: you will need to set aside some time every single day for working on your recovery. The amount of time needed will vary from person to person and many of the tasks you undertake will not be too demanding, and may even be pleasurable.

- **Patience**: there is no miracle cure or magic wand for Anxiety, and in the early stages your progress may feel painfully slow. If you stick with it you will find that you do make progress and it does get easier.

- **Motivation**: how badly do you want to be free of your Anxiety disorder? That is what gives you motivation, and our experience shows that most sufferers have plenty of it.

- **Courage**: you probably don't feel courageous at the moment, but just stop and think. How hard is it to face every day knowing that you might have a panic attack, or that your phobia will haunt you, or your OCD will dominate every moment? Doesn't that take some courage?

- **Support**: many people don't like to admit to having an Anxiety problem, but if you can find someone to support you it will help you through the difficult patches. In Chapter 25 we will give some advice that shows your chosen supporter the best way to help you. An alternative is to make use of one of the helplines that exist for just this purpose – phone numbers are in Appendix 2.

Questionnaire – are you ready for recovery?

How committed are you to recovery?
A bit/quite a lot/100%

How much time can you give each day to the work?
Very little/30 minutes/at least an hour

Are you prepared to wait a while for the results to show?
Yes/No

How do you feel about living with an Anxiety disorder?
Not bothered/fairly unhappy/find it unbearable

Are you ready to face up to what needs to be done?
Yes/No

Have you found a source of support?
Yes/No

Perhaps you found these questions annoying. Did you want to shout 'of course I'm committed and motivated, just show me what to do'? Good. We don't mind if you get angry with us – anger gives you energy, just what you need right now.

Perhaps the hardest thing for many Anxiety sufferers is simply finding the time for a recovery programme. Many Anxiety sufferers are very busy people, juggling family commitments, work and Anxiety in one endless rush. Others are kept busy by their Anxiety – OCD in particular can be very time consuming.

It will be difficult to find enough time at first, but gradually you will turn things around, life will be less fraught, and you will have more time available.

GROUP MEMBERS TALK ABOUT MOVING TOWARDS RECOVERY.

'I just felt relieved. I absolutely believed it, because I knew they'd done all the tests.'
BRIDGET

'I kept going back to the hospital for various things, and eventually I did accept the diagnosis of anxiety.'
JULIE

'As I sat in the Accident and Emergency waiting room ... the situation began to sink in. Here I sat, an acute agoraphobic, prone to panic attacks, unable to walk beyond my own street and I had dealt decisively and efficiently with an emergency. Now, of course, I was wondering how the devil I was going to cope with getting home. It was an extraordinary switch from complete confidence to impending panic...'
MARGARET

'If it were humanly possible to remove every ounce of anxiety from an individual, that person wouldn't survive for very long.'
NORMAN

'My brother died three hours after our mother's funeral. No one was expecting it, we thought it was just a kidney infection. And my boyfriend died in my arms – he had cancer. When these things happened, they didn't make me anxious, they made me stronger. When you're tested like that it's as if someone else takes over and you get through.'
WENDY

6 Two Key Skills: Goal Setting and Relaxation

Key skill – goal setting

Recovery work for Anxiety is based on setting and achieving goals.

Goals need to be realistic

Are you an impatient person? Do you want to rush in and do everything we suggest in the first week? You'll need to curb your enthusiasm. Taking on a goal that is too big for you will lead to failure, and you will feel like giving up. Always make goals small enough that you have a good chance of succeeding. Are you inclined to be over-protective of yourself? In that case, you may need to brace yourself and take a little more risk. Goals that are too small don't provide any challenge and achieving them doesn't bring any reward.

Choose specific goals

Don't say 'my goal is to be happy'. Do say 'my goal is to stop counting my coat hangers' or 'my goal is to post a letter'.

Break goals down into small steps

The answer to both the above difficulties is to break goals down into small steps. Start by choosing an overall goal and then see what smaller goals you could set to help you towards it. The smaller goals can also be broken down – there is an example of how to do this below.

Keep a record of goals and progress

Use your notebook to record the goal and the steps.

Learn from your failures

Counsellors and therapists say that failures are more useful than successes because we learn so much from them. If you fail at one of your goals, don't let yourself plunge into despair. Instead be your own counsellor and try to analyse why you failed – this is the problem that you need to overcome. Rearrange the goal so you have a better chance of success next time.

Repeat your goals

Try to do each goal more than once. Overall it will get easier each time, although there may be the occasional setback.

Example of goal setting – running the marathon

We will give examples of goal setting for Anxiety recovery later on, but for now let's look at an example that has nothing to do with Anxiety. A very unfit person decides to run the marathon to raise money for their favourite charity. A trainer helps them break down their goals.

Main goal

Run the marathon.

Secondary goals

1. Run a mile.
2. Run 5 miles.
3. Run 10 miles.
4. Run a half marathon.

And so on to the actual day of the marathon.

Breakdown of first goal

Since this person is very unfit, there is no way they are going to run even a mile the first time they go training, so they have to work out a series of mini-goals.

1. Walk half a mile on the flat, repeat until comfortable.

2. Walk a mile on the flat, repeat until comfortable.

3. Walk half a mile uphill, repeat until comfortable.

4. Walk a mile uphill, repeat until comfortable.

5. Jog a few yards on the flat, repeat until comfortable.

And so on until they can run a mile.

When setting goals, use the acronym SMART and make your goals:

S = specific (something you can know for sure you'll manage)

M = measurable (something you can rate for success)

A = achievable (something within your ability)

R = relevant (something you want to achieve at this time)

T = timeable (something you can achieve in a specific and short period of time).

Key skill – learning to relax fully

Once you have your tape or CD, or have recorded your own, it's time to start using it. Arrange a time when you won't be disturbed – if there are other people around, explain that you need to be alone for a while. Take the phone off the hook, switch off your mobile.

Lie down, or sit in a comfortable chair, and listen to the recording. Don't try to judge how much you've relaxed, just let it happen. If you fall asleep, that's okay. You can always set an alarm if you need to be up and about at a certain time.

Do this every day. If you are very anxious, do it twice a day, morning and evening. If the recording helps you sleep at night, then use it for that, but don't count that as your session for the day.

Some people find it hard to get started and feel anxious about doing relaxation. Here are some tips:

- The first time you play it, don't try to relax, just listen normally and get used to the voice and the words.

- If you feel very tense and can't sit still while it is playing, then make it your goal to let it run through to the end – anything so long as you play it at least once every day.

- Don't judge yourself if you're finding it hard to relax – some people do, some don't, it's as simple as that.

While you're getting used to relaxation, be prepared to play your recording once or twice a day for at least three weeks. This is to give it a fair chance. It's worth persevering because relaxation is such an important part of recovery.

Once you've formed the habit of doing relaxation every day, keep it up throughout your recovery programme.

GROUP MEMBERS TALK ABOUT RELAXATION

'I do relaxation, I use a CD that the therapist gave me, it has a guided visualisation on it. It sends me to sleep.'
ANDREA

'I don't use relaxation. I've tried it, but I've never developed the discipline. I've always found it hard making the time for it.'
ANDREW

'For a long time I used a relaxation tape, but now I am so familiar with the routine that I can relax myself without a tape. I used the tape 2–3 times a day. I relax in a conscious way at bedtime when I turn the light off. Otherwise whenever I'm aware that my body is tense which would be once to twice a day.'
JULIE

'Regular practice in relaxation techniques... helps you to differentiate between levels of tension and relaxation. If you can recognise when periods of tension appear you will have time to do something about it, before it does something about you.'
NORMAN

'I did practise relaxation while I was in hospital, not so much now although I do use it when I need to. However, I go to local MIND group and they are doing some relaxation. I have some tapes and do some meditation. I've done guided imagery with my therapist but didn't find it so relaxing. I did some aromatherapy and Reiki which were good.'
SARAH

'In the past I've used the progressive muscle relaxation from No Panic, and I do self-hypnosis relaxing all my muscles and it sends me off to sleep.'
WENDY

7 Causes of Anxiety Disorders

Anxiety is experienced by virtually everyone at times. It is a normal and natural feeling when facing situations which are unusual, challenging or risky.

We are all likely to encounter events in our lives which produce anxiety. These may be major such as the death of a close family member or severe financial problems. They can also be the more normal changes which are part of life: changes at work, home or in one's social network. Even going on holiday or preparing for Christmas can involve a measure of anxiety.

A small amount of anxiety is healthy and useful if you are facing something difficult. It helps you to take better care of yourself in a dangerous situation and it can help you perform better, for instance in an exam or public performance.

Abnormal Anxiety is different. It can make you feel excessively afraid in situations that are not stressful or threatening to most people. It can give you such a high level of Anxiety (or nerves) before an event that it stops you thinking or acting in a constructive way.

Anxiety disorders are an extreme development of abnormal Anxiety. If you have an Anxiety disorder, then your anxiety will:

- be more intense than normal
- last longer than normal
- lead you to behave in ways that interfere with your normal life.

How do anxiety disorders develop?

There are various reasons why people develop Anxiety disorders but most sufferers, when they look back, can see that there was a period of stress in their lives that acted as a trigger. In addition, they may feel that they were always nervous, right from childhood, or always tended to worry about things.

Some stages in life seem to make us particularly vulnerable. Adolescence is an obvious one, but many young people seem to go through a difficult time a few years later, shortly after they first leave home. Perhaps life suddenly seems all too serious, with the need to be financially self-sufficient, to look for a partner, and generally establish yourself in the adult world.

But stressful events can strike any of us at any time, and if there are enough of them any one of us can be vulnerable to Anxiety. The Holmes-Rahe Scale was devised to measure stress levels. It is interesting to note that even a pleasurable event such as getting married causes a measurable stress, and could contribute to an Anxiety problem.

Task – measure your stress

Here is a list based on this Scale, and you can use it to measure your stress level. Think back over your life in the two years leading up to your first experience of panic, phobia, obsession or GAD and tick any of the items that you experienced. Add up your score – if it comes to more than 150 then you have experienced more than average stress, and if you score more than 300 then you've had a lot of stress.

Death of a spouse	100	Trouble with in-laws	29
Divorce	73	Big personal achievement	28
Marital separation	65	Spouse starts/stops work	26
Imprisonment	63	Start/stop school	26
Death of close relative	63	Living conditions change	24
Personal injury/illness	53	Personal habits change	24
Marriage	50	Trouble with boss	23
Dismissal from work	47	Work hours/conditions change	20
Marital reconciliation	45	Moving house	20
Retirement	45	Change school	19
Change in health of relative	44	Change recreation	19
Pregnancy	40	Alter Church activities	19
Sexual difficulties	39	Alter social activities	18
New family member	39	Small mortgage/loan	17
Business readjustment	39	Alter sleeping habits	16
Financial change	38	Change in family reunions	15
Change in marital rows	35	Alter eating habits	15
Major mortgage	32	Holidays	13
Foreclosure of mortgage/loan	30	Christmas	12
Work responsibilities change	29	Minor law breaking	11
Child leaves home	29		

Don't dismiss this. People will often say 'yes, but I should have been able to cope'. There is no should about it.

GROUP MEMBERS TALK ABOUT THE BUILD-UP TO ANXIETY

'I had a "naughty" magazine which was not unreasonable for a boy of 11. I knew I should not have it so I would hide it. But being so scared it would be discovered I found that I had to keep going to it to make sure it was there, to make sure that I had actually hidden it.'
ANDREW

'At the time there were some concerns around my blood pressure and I was feeling quite anxious about it. I was under stress at work.'
BRIDGET

'My first bout of anxiety was triggered by a relationship break up – I suffered from depression first and then anxiety followed.'
JULIE

'Our eldest son ... developed acute bronchitis ... my husband was having regular attacks of fever. I was walking home alone ... the road seemed to be undulating ... heaving like the waves of the sea ... the garden walls were leaning towards me ... my heart started to beat rapidly ... my vision was becoming blurred ... there was a thumping beat in my head and I couldn't breathe.'
MARGARET

'There was a long slow build up to my first bout of anxiety. Four years before I had a severe ear infection that led to balance problems, which was very frightening and went on for 10 months. This was followed over the next couple of years by my degree finals, a divorce and worries about getting a job.'
PEN

'I know now that it all started at the dentist when I was 13, I wasn't scared of the dentist but they locked the door, and I panicked, they pushed me down on the chair and three of them held me while they put the gas mask on my face.'
WENDY

8 The Connection between Mind, Body and Spirit

We are complicated creatures. Mind, body and spirit are all inter-connected, and can influence each other in ways that we often fail to understand.

Very often when a person is told that they have an Anxiety disorder they find it hard to believe. Their symptoms feel so physical, so they are sure there must be something physically wrong. All their tests are negative, but somehow they can't believe it. Surely this racing heart, these shaking legs, this churning stomach, can't all be down to my mind playing tricks?

On the other hand, a person tormented by obsessive thoughts can find it hard to believe that there is any physical element to their suffering. How can doing more exercise or improving sleep patterns have an effect on my thoughts?

If you have either of those reactions to your diagnosis, just stop and think for a moment. Think back to the time before you had Anxiety.

When you were happy, did you smile or laugh?
When you were upset, did you cry?
When you were worried, did you feel like there was a weight in your chest?
When you were nervous, did you get butterflies in your stomach?

You are aware of your emotions in your mind, and yet your body feels them too, and expresses them. If you know someone well, you can tell just from their body language what mood they're in.

Or look at it another way:

Why does jaunty music make us want to tap our toes?

Why do we sit on the edge of our seat watching an exciting movie?

Why does that person chew their lip when they're thinking?

Whenever your mind is active, your body seems to want to express what's going on. This means that it's perfectly possible for mental distress to cause physical symptoms and for physical care to soothe mental anguish.

Values and beliefs

Spiritual matters are harder to explain, but they affect our minds and our bodies equally. As human beings we want to do more than just survive and raise our children in safety. We want fulfilment and a sense of purpose.

If you've ever been in love, you know how that affects you physically, and that you just don't notice little aches and pains. Scientists tell us that the experience of love releases chemicals called endorphins that make us feel good and block pain.

Similarly, someone with deeply held beliefs will feel stronger physically and happier in themselves.

This doesn't mean that anyone with an Anxiety disorder will need to be religious before they can recover, but it does mean that you will need to look at that aspect of your life, and make sure that you are giving yourself what you need.

Understanding more about your body

Your brain and your body communicate with each other via your nervous system. If you hit your thumb with a hammer, your nerves carry messages about that to your brain and you feel pain (and probably say something unprintable too). Your brain sends messages back to your body so that it can start the process of healing the damage you've just done to yourself.

A similar process happens if you are frightened. Something scary happens, your brain reacts, and sends messages to your body. But why those particular messages, the ones that make your heart thump and your stomach churn?

The answer is that the whole system evolved a very long time ago, when primitive people were living lives filled with physical danger. Dangerous animals, floods, forest fires, and of course people on the warpath were all sources of danger. And without all the contrivances of modern life people usually only had two choices when confronted with danger: fight back, or run away.

Both of these options require physical energy. You need to pump more oxygen to your arms and legs if you are going to fight, or run. You need to stop digesting your dinner, make swift decisions, move quickly.

And this is why, when you are very anxious or panicky, your heart races, your limbs tremble, you need the loo, your head swims and you simply can't bear to stay in one place.

The fact that you are frightened of something that doesn't present any physical danger to you is neither here nor there to the primitive system that takes charge at that moment. You are frightened, and without hesitation your brain and your body prepare you for fight or flight.

Recovery largely consists of finding ways to first tolerate the sensations and then turn off the fight-or-flight system. However, fight-or-flight is controlled by your involuntary nervous system. As the name suggests, you have no conscious control over it.

Changing your breathing

There is an exception to most rules, and in the case of your nervous system the exception is breathing. Breathing is automatic and is controlled by your involuntary nervous system but at the same time we do have a certain amount of control over it.

You can choose to hold your breath, or to pant like a dog. Athletes, singers and actors use breath control to improve their performance. People who do yoga or meditation work with their breathing as part of the process.

During a panic attack, most people feel that their breathing is wildly out of control. They feel the need to suck in great gulps of air, as if they can't get enough, and often feel unable to breathe out fully before taking the next breath in. In fact doing this only fuels the panic attack and makes it worse.

This is because it is all part of the fight-or-flight mechanism. The extra oxygen that you are taking in is being rushed to your muscles to pump them up ready for action. If you are in a situation where you don't need to take any physical action, such as in a queue or driving a car, then that oxygen will stay in your system and add to your uncomfortable sensations.

It doesn't help that concerned companions will often advise you to 'take a deep breath'. They may be worried that you are about to faint (you may be worried about that too) but in fact you don't need any more breath, you already have too much.

In a panic attack breathing becomes very noticeable, but many Anxiety sufferers tend to breathe in an unhelpful way most of the time. Anxiety makes you tense, and tension make you breathe in a shallow, fast way, using only the top half of your chest. This means that you are probably taking in more oxygen than you need, and you are not breathing out all of the carbon dioxide. The stale air at the bottom of your lungs is never properly cleared out.

The result of this can be a permanent light-headed feeling, and fatigue. Changing your breathing habits is an important part of Anxiety recovery.

Key skill – breathing exercise one

We will have more to say about breathing later, but for now here is a simple technique to practise. Start by doing this exercise when you are sitting comfortably and when you are not particularly anxious. Practise it a few times and take note of how it feels and how it affects your body. This is so that you can learn to trust this type of breathing. You need to know that it won't make you feel any worse.

1. Take a normal breath in.
2. When you breathe out, try to make that breath last longer than the breath in.
3. Do this for several breaths, rhythmically.
4. Take a break.

If you find it hard to establish a rhythm with this new kind of breathing, try counting in your head.

1. Breathe in to a count of 4.
2. Breathe out to a count of 8.
3. Do this for several breaths.
4. Take a break.

If these counts are too long for you, then choose your own numbers. If you can manage longer counts, then do so. The slower and calmer your breathing becomes, the better.

Once you feel comfortable breathing like this, you can do it as often as you like. It won't hurt you, in fact it will help you. In particular, use it when you are in a situation that is difficult for you, where you might panic or become very anxious. Start the breathing as early as possible, so that you go into the situation calmly.

GROUP MEMBERS TALK ABOUT BREATHING

'I don't work on my breathing, I find that really difficult. Just thinking about it makes it go haywire.'
ANDREA

'I have worked on my breathing – it's the most important thing for me. I use a computer programme that monitors heart rhythms and it shows you the importance of regular even breathing for coherence. The speed of breathing isn't important; what helps me is the awareness of the rhythm of my breathing.'
ANDREW

'I know that I breathe badly when I'm tense, I need to work on that.'
BRIDGET

'I learnt how to control my breathing and I've found this really helpful. I tried various techniques and the one that was easiest for me was to breathe in to a count of 4, hold my breath for 4 and breathe out to a count of 6. Now that I'm so used to it I don't need to count, and I just breathe slowly and evenly through the nose and from the abdomen, breathing out for slightly longer than I breathe in.'
JULIE

'I was told it was best to breathe 10–12 times a minute and I had to learn to slow down by timing myself with a stopwatch. I still monitor my breathing on bad days and now it's much slower!'
PEN

'I've worked on my breathing – the hospital taught me to blow bubbles. It forces my breathing to slow down and makes me concentrate, which reduces the anxiety.'
SARAH

'I breathe in for four and out for four, I do it when I'm getting anxious.'
WENDY

9 Taking Exercise to Help Anxiety

Remember to check with your doctor before starting an exercise programme.

As well as daily relaxation, you will need to take exercise as part of your recovery programme – but the good news is, you won't have to run a marathon! Exercise is helpful in several ways:

- It helps burn off muscle tension.
- It helps healthy breathing.
- It produces beneficial chemicals in your brain.
- It helps convince you that your body is strong enough to cope with your Anxiety symptoms.

The most useful kind of exercise is aerobic exercise – that is, something that gets you out of breath. You need to do it for at least 20 minutes before the chemicals are released. This means that you get most benefit from taking exercise three times a week for at least 20 minutes each time.

Many Anxiety sufferers lose the habit of taking exercise, and some become extremely inactive. Some forms of Anxiety, such as compulsive behaviours, are very time consuming, and other types of Anxiety can leave the sufferer feeling too exhausted to contemplate taking exercise. This is a vicious circle, because the less you use your body, the less you feel like using it.

And your body was designed to be used – this means doing exercise that is appropriate for each individual. Even people with physical health problems can usually find a type of exercise that is within their capacity – your doctor should be able to advise you about this. Many forms of exercise are taken outdoors, in the fresh air and in natural surroundings, and there is some evidence that this is good for our mental health (but see below for exercise tips for housebound people).

Set your sights as low as you need to. If you have been spending all your time in the armchair, locked into Anxiety, then start by walking about the room a little at regular intervals. Or if you are active but don't take exercise, start with something gentle like a walk in a park. It doesn't matter how long it takes you to reach the 20 minutes three times a week target – just make a start.

Exercise options

It's surprising how many Anxiety sufferers say that they 'always hated games at school'. If that's you, then you have an extra level of challenge, but remember, there's plenty of things you can do that are nothing like school games.

If you're an exercise hater, then try some lateral thinking. Any vigorous activity counts, as long as it makes you breathe hard – scrub a floor, run up some stairs, swing your arms about. You don't have to do sports, and you don't have to join a gym. You just have to get active. You could also try:

● walking, especially in the countryside or a park
● jogging
● line dancing
● swimming
● aerobics (there are special classes for the over-50s)
● social dancing
● country dancing
● cycling.

Start with one activity once a week, and add others so that you don't grow bored.

What if you're housebound?

It can seem impossibly hard to take exercise if your Anxiety has made you housebound, but in fact there are plenty of options. Tell yourself that one day you will be able to go out and take part in other activities, and exercising in the house is part of your training for that goal. Here are some suggestions:

- walk round the house or flat
- go up and down stairs, if available
- do housework
- use an exercise video or DVD
- use an exercise bike, or treadmill.

If you are using an exercise video or DVD, try to find one that is not too challenging. They always start with a warm-up session, and at first that is all you should attempt. Slowly increase the amount of time you are able to exercise and don't attempt anything that is too much for you. If you open the window while you are exercising you'll benefit even more.

Establishing a personal exercise programme

It doesn't matter how active or inactive you are, you can start improving your fitness with a structured exercise programme. Look at the graduated exercise ladder below and decide where you are on it. Be honest with yourself, no one else needs to know about it.

Exercise ladder

Stand up, walk round the room
  Walk up and down stairs
    Exercise video or DVD – warm-up
      Exercise video or DVD – complete
        Exercise machine or activity of choice – once a week
          Exercise machine or activity – twice a week
            Exercise machine or activity – three times a week

When you have placed yourself on the ladder, use your goal-setting skills to work out how to move on to the next rung of the ladder. You may not feel able to make the move in one jump – that's fine, you can break it down into a series of small steps.

Here's an example for someone who is trying to move on to 20 minutes of exercise once a week but whose chosen activity doesn't quite fit with that.

GOAL: join Beginners Ballroom Dance class.

PROBLEM: class lasts an hour, I don't feel fit enough for that yet.

SOLUTION: further repeats of exercise video/DVD until I can exercise for an hour, plus a graded series of walks outside building up to an hour.

GROUP MEMBERS TALK ABOUT EXERCISE

'Exercise helps me a lot, at first I was too ill to do much but now I walk every day, between 2 and 6 miles, and I spend half an hour on my exercise bike.'
ANDREA

'It does help me to take exercise. Exercise has a way of taking that ball of tangled string that's your mind and untangling it. It's something about the steady rhythm that soothes me. I like to use a treadmill or a bike.'
ANDREW

'I don't feel that exercise helps me because I don't enjoy any kind of adrenaline rush – it feels like I'm losing control. I do love to swim, because I find it calming and I like to go 3 or 4 times a week, but if I'm anxious I don't enjoy it and I don't feel it works. So I don't use exercise as a recovery tool, but it does help me to maintain good mental health.'
JULIE

'Exercise helps. I go jogging and go to the gym, walk, cycle. At one time I exercised too much and it made me ill, but it helps to go for a run or a walk to take my mind off anxious thoughts. Doctors have told me about serotonin and endorphins. It really does help me.'
SARAH

10 Examining Your Diet

Task – recording what you eat

Use your notebook to keep a record of everything you eat and drink for a few days. Write down the time of day as well as what you have. Here's an example:

TIME   FOOD/DRINK
07.30   Tea with milk and two sugars
09.00   Biscuit
12.30   Cheese sandwich, apple

and so on through the day.

You don't have to make a precise record of quantities, because this isn't a weight loss, or weight gain, exercise.

Food and drink

Somebody who is well nourished will feel stronger and more able to face life's challenges, and yet Anxiety often brings with it a lack of appetite, or a desire to eat comfort foods that may have little nutritional value.

Many of us are drawn to sugary foods, such as cakes, sweets, biscuits and chocolate. They taste nice and give us a quick fix by producing a little burst of energy. This is because of the effect the sugar has on blood sugar levels. Unfortunately it wears off just as quickly, leaving you down in the dumps again.

What's more, a sudden change in blood sugar can make you feel a bit light headed or shaky, which is the last feeling you need if you're on the alert for the next panic attack.

The natural sugar (or fructose) that occurs in fruit doesn't have this effect on your body. Because of the way your body processes fructose it doesn't cause a big increase in blood sugar or the sudden drop in blood sugar that follows. This means that eating fruit can satisfy your sweet tooth without having a bad effect on your Anxiety.

When you have kept a record for a week or so, compare it with the model below.

Model
(this model is for Anxiety management, not nutrition or weight loss)

Eat something within 20 minutes of waking up – remember your body will have been without food for several hours overnight. This doesn't have to be a full breakfast, but once you are fully awake it is good to eat breakfast – it will give you energy for the next few hours.

Have a snack mid-morning, a light lunch, another snack mid-afternoon and an evening meal, then finally a snack before bedtime. In other words, eat little and often throughout the day and keep the night time fast as short as possible. If you are worried about being overweight, then make your meals smaller so that you can have snacks.

Avoid cakes, biscuits, sweets and sugary drinks both at mealtimes and for snacks. Snacks can be fresh fruit, milky drinks or dried fruit and nuts. If you have a really sweet tooth, then have a dessert after your main meal – because you have eaten a meal, the sweet food won't have such a dramatic effect on your blood sugar. Here's an example:

TIME	FOOD/DRINK
07.30	Cereal with milk and sugar
08.15	Fruit smoothie
11.30	Fruit juice, apple
13.00	Water, tuna sandwich, yoghurt
15.00	Decaffeinated coffee, handful of raisins
17.00	Water, apple
19.30	Stir-fried chicken, almonds and bean sprouts, rice, stewed apple
21.00	Banana

If you have a very active lifestyle you may need to eat more than this, or less if you are very sedentary. This is just an example to show you how you can eat little and often through the day. You can eat the kind of food you like.

Your eating pattern

How does your eating pattern compare with the model? If it is very different, don't despair, a series of small changes will gradually help you – you can use your goal setting skills to break the changes up so that they are manageable.

Breakfast is important

One very common problem for many Anxiety sufferers is the feeling that they can't face breakfast. They may wait several hours before eating anything and in extreme cases will only eat once a day, in the evening when they feel up to it. This creates a vicious circle, because someone whose system is very empty is bound to feel lethargic and even slightly unwell, which makes them less likely to eat, and by not eating they feel even worse, and so on.

In the example above, there is a 10½ hour gap between the last snack of the day and the first one of the next day. After such a long wait your body needs fuel to get it going. If you skip breakfast you're denying it that fuel and yet you need energy to start your day. What is your body to do? One answer is to pump adrenalin into your system – not a good idea for someone with Anxiety.

Since breakfast is the most important meal of the day it is worth trying to manage it. Try some lateral thinking – breakfast doesn't have to be cereal, toast or eggs and bacon. How about a banana or some yoghurt? If the only thing you can face is a sweet biscuit, then break the sugary snacks rule and have biscuits. When you've got used to eating breakfast you can switch to something healthier.

Also, no one likes to waste food, and yet for someone who is struggling a whole banana or a whole slice of toast can seem just too much. The answer is that while you are working on your recovery you can let go of feelings of guilt about food wastage. The most important thing is for you to recover, so if you only want a piece of banana or a spoonful of yoghurt tell yourself it's okay.

This applies to other meals. Eat what you can, in the quantities you can manage. Try to eat a little something at each mealtime and snack time. The way you eat is also important. Allow time to eat your meals calmly and without rushing.

Your body will gradually adjust to the new regime, your energy levels will rise and the vicious circle will be broken.

GROUP MEMBERS TALK ABOUT FOOD AND DRINK

'I do occasionally skip breakfast but I can't remember if I did on the day of the panic attack.'
BRIDGET

'When my anxiety was bad I used to skip meals and eat when I could face it, so of course I often had low blood sugar and that made me feel worse. Also I had a very restricted diet as I bought all my food from the milkman.'
JULIE

'In later years I wondered if the fact that I was so anaemic had had a bearing on the beginnings of my anxiety problems.'
MARGARET

'I've always eaten sensibly but I do become hypoglycaemic when I'm nervous. I need to keep my blood sugar steady.'
PEN

'I have had binges on sugary foods, sometimes gets out of control even to the point were I make myself sick. I am now trying to find healthier, more positive outlets.'
SARAH

'I've always eaten well, when I was on Valium I didn't put on any weight at all, I was constantly hungry but I was underweight.'
WENDY

11 More about Diet

Understanding the effects of caffeine

Caffeine is a mild stimulant that raises your heart rate and creates a short-lived burst of energy. That is why so many people avoid coffee in the evenings – it keeps them awake. Anxiety uses up a lot of a person's energy and so caffeine can seem like an absolute boon, but for some people it is a false friend, because they are already over-stimulated. Too much caffeine can also trigger panic attacks or make you more susceptible to them. Also people vary in their sensitivity to caffeine, so that some feel an almost miraculous change when they give it up, whereas others feel there is little difference.

Take a look at the food and drink records you kept for the exercise above, and count up the caffeine based drinks you have in an average day. Caffeine is found in tea, coffee, most cola drinks and energy drinks. If you are having more than two or three caffeine drinks a day it would be worth cutting down, or even better, giving up altogether.

Do it gradually, because stopping suddenly can give you a withdrawal headache and a few days of feeling mildly unwell. (Of course for anyone who does experience this, it is a sure sign that they are sensitive to caffeine and would be better off without it). Try cutting out every other drink, or make your drinks smaller. Make sure you keep your fluid levels up by substituting water, milk or fruit juice. Give yourself at least two weeks to give up caffeine, making small changes each day.

Once you have stopped having caffeine you need to maintain that throughout your Anxiety recovery programme. You may feel some immediate benefit, but the greatest improvements happen quite slowly. Those people who are very sensitive to caffeine would be best to give it up permanently.

Checklist – food and drink

It's time to look at your eating and drinking habits and decide where you might benefit from making changes. Use the checklist to help you focus – any box that you can't tick is one that you can choose to work on.

- ☐ eating something within 20 minutes of waking up
- ☐ breakfast, either then or not long after
- ☐ mid-morning snack
- ☐ lunch
- ☐ mid-afternoon snack
- ☐ dinner
- ☐ light supper
- ☐ avoiding sweets and chocolate
- ☐ avoiding cakes and biscuits
- ☐ avoiding caffeine
- ☐ eating fresh fruit and vegetables
- ☐ eating a wide variety of foods
- ☐ drinking plenty of water

Use your goal setting skills to make these changes.

Compare your diaries

Once you have a set of records for both your Anxiety and your food and drink intake then you can compare them. Look to see if there is a pattern.

Ask yourself:

- Is my Anxiety worst when my system is empty?

- Does my Anxiety go up after a caffeine-based drink, or after eating sweets or biscuits?

- Do I feel calmer after a meal?

For some people the link is very strong, and it can come as quite a shock to realise how much impact poor eating habits can have on Anxiety.

GROUP MEMBERS TALK ABOUT CAFFEINE

'I've never felt that caffeine was a factor in my anxiety – I have tried cutting down and it made no difference, although I am aware of the effects if I have too much coffee.'
ANDREW

'I gave up caffeine and it helped me quite a lot.'
JULIE

'I know I drink too much coffee. I started because I was on medication which made me tired. Now I am off the medication that made me so tired but drinking too much coffee has become a habit. Also took caffeine pills – I used to get very anxious around bedtime because of nightmares, so I wanted to keep awake. I overdosed on the pills and they made me feel sick, also anxiety increased because I was worried about getting sick and the fact that I had too much caffeine in my system.'
SARAH

'I've never worried about caffeine, and I like the sugar in a coffee. If I'm out sometimes I have a coffee, I feel I need the sugar. You've got to find out what suits you.'
WENDY

12 Understanding Alcohol, Nicotine and Other Drugs

Alcohol

Many anxious people resort to alcohol in the belief that it helps them cope with stressful situations. Unfortunately alcohol is a depressant, and therefore not helpful to Anxiety sufferers. Examine your records from the exercise above and be honest with yourself about the amount of alcohol you consume – could you, for instance, go a whole week without an alcoholic drink? If the answer is yes, then take alcohol out of your diet for a week just to prove that you can. Once you've done that, you can allow yourself occasional social drinks during your recovery.

If the answer is no, then it is time to seek help and to find a way to give up alcohol. This needs to be done before embarking on Anxiety recovery, because, unfortunately, alcohol used like this covers up the anxious feelings, and you need to be able to experience them, in a controlled way, in order to deal with them.

This is also why you should never use alcohol to get you through an Anxiety provoking situation – you may feel pleased that you managed it, but, in fact, you learnt nothing and you may have started a very bad habit indeed.

Nicotine

As well as being bad for your general health, smoking has a bad effect on Anxiety – nicotine is a stimulant that actually raises Anxiety levels. However we all know that giving up smoking is a major project in its own right, and someone with very bad Anxiety may simply not feel up to the challenge. If you choose to work on your Anxiety first, promise yourself that giving up cigarettes will be the next thing that you tackle. In the meantime, cut down as far as you possibly can and in particular never smoke on an empty stomach.

Prescription drugs

People who become addicted to prescription drugs can experience Anxiety symptoms when they try to withdraw from them. Tranquillisers (or benzodiazepines) are the most commons source of this difficulty. At one time they were prescribed without a full understanding of the side effects of long-term usage. In fact once your body becomes used to them, you can start to feel Anxiety symptoms while you are still taking them, and these can become worse as you try to withdraw from the drugs.

The answer is to withdraw gradually and with support from a trained professional. All of the techniques used for managing Anxiety will be useful, but you will have to allow the time for your body to get used to the reduction in your dosage. See Extra Information 3 for more on this.

If you are taking other prescription drugs check with your doctor about any side effects that might be causing you to feel anxious.

Street drugs

If you are addicted to street drugs this may well be a factor in your Anxiety, but your primary concern is to deal with the addiction problem. If you are a casual user and you have developed Anxiety, then it's time to stop. Like alcohol, nicotine and caffeine, street drugs will either give you an energy burst that soon wears off, or mask the anxious feelings, making it impossible for you to work on them.

You need to be honest with yourself and decide if you need to deal with any drug problems before you start work on your Anxiety recovery. Use the following guidelines to help you decide:

- If you are a smoker, then you will be able to make progress with your Anxiety recovery.

- If you are using alcohol to blanket the anxious feelings, then you are unlikely to achieve any progress.

- If your problems are caused or made worse by prescription drugs, then you will be able to make progress, but expect it to be slow. You should check with your GP before starting self-help.

- If you are using street drugs you should give them up before starting on Anxiety recovery.

Set your goals

Use the checklist below to assess your exposure to various drugs.

Nicotine	Per day
Alcohol	Per day
	Per week
Prescription drugs	Per day
	Check with GP about side effects
Street drugs	Per day
	Per week

GROUP MEMBERS TALK ABOUT ALCOHOL, NICOTINE AND OTHER DRUGS

'I used to smoke, up to 50 a day. I thought it helped with anxiety but now know it doesn't and I saw the effects on long-term smokers on the ward in hospital. I quit a year and a half ago, now feel healthier though still anxious but now I don't have the added anxiety of "needing a tab" (cigarette).'

'I used to drink but very rarely do now, as I am calorie conscious. I know I get more irrational when I drink and can act impulsively.'

'I smoked cannabis when I was 15 but have not touched it since I was 16. It made me more paranoid and anxious though I didn't realise it at the time.'

SARAH

'I do smoke, when I gave it up I got colds all the time. When I had anxiety badly I never drank at all, my mother used to say "what do you want to drink for, it does you no good at all", but now I like one drink in the evening.'

WENDY

13 Your Sleep Patterns

Sleep can become a major worry for people with Anxiety. Some people find it hard to get enough sleep because their mind is racing and their body on full alert. Others are so exhausted from the constant tension of Anxiety that they sleep for much longer than they normally would.

These are sleep problems which can be dealt with as part of your Anxiety recovery programme. There are also sleep disorders, such as sleep apnoea, which need medical help. If you suspect that you have a sleep disorder, then you should talk to your doctor. If you're not sure you could try the self-help methods that we suggest first and see if they help.

Worrying about sleep

As with most aspects of Anxiety, sleep problems can form a vicious circle.

Tension and worry can affect the amount or quality of sleep you get, but lack of sleep in turn reduces your energy and ability to cope the following day. This builds up more Anxiety, making for another bad night, and so on. Also, with certain types of Anxiety, worry about not sleeping itself becomes part of the problem.

Similarly, dozing on the couch all day and sleeping through the night can actually leave you feeling lethargic and without any energy, so that you want to do the same thing the next day. Worrying that you aren't strong enough to stay awake all day only adds to the problem.

We tend to think in terms of eight hours a night, but this is only a rough guide, and people vary in their sleep needs. We are programmed to sleep when it is dark and to be active when it is daylight, so we may sleep more in winter. Also some activities are more tiring than others, so that we sleep more some nights than others.

Task – deal with your sleep

Start by keeping a sleep diary for a couple of weeks – use your notebook to record when you sleep, and how long for.

Make a note if you take a long time to get to sleep, if you wake up frequently during the night, if you wake up in the early hours and can't get back to sleep.

Make a note of the times you sleep during the day, even if it's only a cat nap.

Once you have a record of your sleep over a period of time you can examine it to see if there is a pattern. If you are worried about lack of sleep, check to see that this really is the case – you may be surprised at how much sleep you're getting.

Compare your diaries

Since you are already keeping an Anxiety diary you can compare the two and see if there is a connection. Do you sleep less after a bad day for Anxiety, or does the exhaustion mean that you sleep more?

When you are lying awake, are you troubled by anxious thoughts and/or physical symptoms of Anxiety? Do you have dreams or nightmares? Do you have some good nights and some bad, and are they connected to anything which has happened in the day? Or to the weather, temperature in the bedroom, time you go to bed, what you have eaten or drunk before bedtime?

If you are troubled by anxious thoughts, either while you are settling down to sleep, or when you wake during the night, you will need to devise a strategy for dealing with them. In Part Three you will learn how Anxiety affects your thinking, and learn some techniques for reducing anxious thoughts. In the meantime, put the rest of the sleep programme in place so that you start to form good habits. The next step is to see what changes you can make to improve matters. It's largely a question of training yourself and, of course, being patient while you wait for the changes to take effect. Use the checklist below to make sure you've done as much as possible.

- ☐ Make sure your bedroom is as comfortable and peaceful as possible. Don't use the room for anything else – remove any TVs, computers and other distractions.
- ☐ Make sure the room is at the right temperature for you, and is well ventilated – open the window during the day to let fresh air in.
- ☐ Make sure the bed is comfortable, with clean warm bedding and a supportive mattress. (If you can't afford a new mattress, try putting a board under the old one.)
- ☐ Make sure the room is dark enough for you – if the curtains or blinds let in light, then add linings or buy blackout blinds. If you prefer a little light that's fine.
- ☐ Decide how long you need to sleep for, and add a little time for your preferred before sleep activity (reading, sex, relaxation etc). Tell yourself that is all the time you will spend in bed.
- ☐ Have a wind-down period of at least half an hour before you get ready for bed. Complete any chores or tasks, let phone calls go to voicemail and spend the time with some relaxing activity.
- ☐ Do not have a heavy meal within three hours of going to bed (make your supper something light). Avoid drinks containing caffeine and alcohol.
- ☐ If you can't get to sleep within 30 minutes of going to bed or of waking up in the night, don't stay in bed – get up and go into another room and do something calming and relaxing until you feel sleepy.
- ☐ If you are sleeping a lot, consider reducing the amount of sleep you have during the day. Do this slowly and allow yourself to get used to each reduction. Also try going to bed later and getting up earlier.

GROUP MEMBERS TALK ABOUT SLEEP

'When I'm very anxious I can't get to sleep because of the thoughts going round and round.'
ANDREA

'I've always slept well. I do feel anxious when I wake up though.'
ANDREW

'When I'm anxious I don't sleep at all, and if I do fall asleep I get terrible nightmares.'
JULIE

'I don't suffer from insomnia, when I'm anxious I tend to sleep too much.'
PEN

'I still get nightmares but I am getting better, not so scared of them. I don't take sleeping pills. I try not to drink too much coffee at night. Exercising helps with my sleeping.'
SARAH

'I wake up if I'm anxious.'
WENDY

14 Positive Experiences

Anxiety sucks all the pleasure out of life. It can seem as if you'll never be able to just enjoy yourself again. If you make a conscious effort to find positive and enjoyable experiences you can start to turn this around. Don't wait till happiness comes to you – seek it out.

Think about all the things that used to give you pleasure before you had Anxiety. Some of them will be too difficult right now because of your Anxiety, but there may be something – a hobby, an interest – that you can still pursue. Tell yourself that you'll go back to the other things when you're better, and that in the meantime you'll enjoy those things you can still do.

Or you may want to try something new – something quieter and less challenging perhaps than your previous activities. Again you can always promise yourself you'll go back to your old interests when you're better.

There are some things that are good for all of us. Try to find a way of giving yourself something out of each of the following categories.

The value of laughter

Research has showed that laughing is good for us, both mentally and physically. Mentally, it releases chemicals in the brain that make us feel happier, and physically it frees up muscle tension. There is even some evidence that you don't have to actually be amused to benefit – just laughing for no reason can be beneficial. There are laughter groups where people meet just to practise laughing.

It's easier though if you find something genuinely funny. Humour is all around us, all you have to do is plug into it. Choose one or more things from the list and give a few minutes every day to it:

- Watch a funny DVD or TV programme.
- Listen to comedy on the radio, or on a CD.
- Read cartoons, in a newspaper or book.
- Read a humorous novel.
- Find jokes on the internet.

Social contacts

We are social creatures. Isolation isn't good for us, and yet Anxiety can be a very isolating experience. If it is at all possible for you to socialise with other people, then do so. Seek out those people who you feel most comfortable with and enjoy their company.

If your Anxiety causes you social difficulties then don't torture yourself by attempting this one – it's meant to be a pleasure, not a pain.

Getting out into the fresh air

Most of us live in crowded urban environments, and yet we evolved in the wide open spaces of Africa. It's no wonder that we find cities stressful, and that we benefit from being outside where there is grass and sky.

If you have a garden, spend as much time in it as possible. If you can, go for a walk in a park, or in the open countryside.

When you look at the horizon, your eye muscles are fully relaxed and this helps you to relax your head and neck – this is one reason why most of us enjoy being by the sea. So if you can get somewhere where there is a good view into the distance, go for it.

Animals

There is evidence that stroking and interacting with a pet has a similar effect to laughing. If you have a pet, spend quality time with it every day. If there are no animals in your household, have any of your friends and family got an obliging cat or dog? Could you offer to help out at your local animal rescue centre?

If your anxiety is in anyway focused on animals, don't undertake this, although you might want to set goals around it during your recovery.

GROUP MEMBERS TALK ABOUT POSITIVE EXPERIENCES

'I like to see humour in everyday situations and I love to laugh and smile.'
ANDREW

'Because I know I can listen to music, or go for a run, I won't sit around letting the anxious thoughts take hold. If I didn't already have these things in place, I wouldn't be motivated to do them when I'm feeling anxious. I take part in charity events, and did the Race for Life. Training for these events provides a focus to keep up my fitness. And a great sense of achievement once I had completed them.'
SARAH

---

15 Achieving Life Balance and Managing Your Time

Anxiety disorders often develop after a period of stress in your life, and if your score in Chapter 7 was higher than 150 then this is likely to be the case for you.

On the other hand, there are some people who don't have enough stress in their lives, and their Anxiety can get out of control because they have too much time to brood about things. (If this seems like a strange concept, try changing the word 'stress' to 'challenge'. A life without any challenges is a life without stimulus, which leads to boredom.)

Whatever your situation, you will need to look at the overall balance of your life and make sure that it is healthy, and that you are getting what you need.

At times of stress we all tend to ignore our own needs and focus on the things that need to be done. If someone is ill and needs our help, if there is a rush on at work, after a death or during any other stressful event, our instincts take over and get us through it.

When the crisis is over, we breathe a sigh of relief and assume that things will soon get back to normal. This is the very time when someone is likely to have their first panic attack, or some other symptom of Anxiety. It can seem so unfair to find yourself having to deal with this when you've already had so much on your plate, and specially when you were looking forward to a bit of peace and quiet.

Why anxiety strikes after a stressful event

There are two reasons why this tends to happen.

1. During the crisis, the chemicals that are circulating in your body are designed to get you through. They include adrenalin, but you need that adrenalin. It gives you the energy to manage the extra load caused by the crisis. As well as physical energy, you need mental energy, and if you are focusing on coping with the here and now you won't have any time for brooding and worrying.

2. When the crisis is over, you are released from the need to deal with the immediate problems. You may still be flooded with adrenalin, which you no longer need, and your mind will start to process what has happened and react to it.

You can't do anything about point number 1. – in fact you need that ability to rise to the moment, it's a very important human characteristic. The answer to point number 2. is to learn to look after yourself, to nurture yourself, after the stress is over.

For many people an Anxiety disorder is the price they pay for not caring for themselves properly. It's as if a small voice inside you has been asking for your attention, and when you ignore that voice it eventually decides to yell and shout, by hitting you with a panic attack, phobia or compulsion.

Despite this, many people feel guilty about taking care of themselves. They put their work, their family, their chores at home ahead of their own needs. Are you one of them? There is no need to feel guilty about looking after yourself – if you do this, you will be more able to look after others.

The same is true if your life is without challenges. If you don't have money worries, or physical health worries, and if everything you want is right there for you, you could well feel guilty about acknowledging that you still aren't happy. After all, so many other people have it much tougher than you. But knowing that doesn't make you feel any better, does it? And it doesn't make your Anxiety go away. Just like someone who has too much stress, you need to make changes so that you can get better. Feeling guilty is just a waste of energy.

Assessing your life balance

Use your notebook to keep a record of how you spend your time for a complete week. You will soon see if you are leaving any time for your own needs. Here is an example of a day from a working parent's notebook:

07.30   get up, shower, breakfast, make packed lunches, drop kids at school
09.15   late to work again, better skip lunch
17.30   leave work, pick up shopping, take oldest child to activity
19.00   eat with partner and kids, my turn to wash up
20.00   my turn to put kids to bed, usual arguments
21.00   check emails, phone childminder re school holidays, organize Badminton Club fixture list, online banking, phone Mum, mend broken door in kitchen
23.00   bed

Not much time for self in there. Some days just are very busy of course, but if the whole diary was like this, then this person would need to think things through and make changes. How hard it would be if they were also struggling with an Anxiety disorder, and yet this is exactly what many people are having to do.

In the example above, the following changes might be possible even on this busy day:

● Show the children how to make their own lunch, under supervision, leaving more time for the journey to school and work. Then it won't be necessary to skip lunch, and the lunch break can become a small window of rest in the busy day.

- Work out why bedtime causes arguments, and try to make it more enjoyable.

- Ask someone else to take over the fixture list.

You may still feel that you haven't really got time for yourself, but as a part of your recovery from Anxiety you need to find some time every day for yourself. It can be something as simple as a relaxing bath, watching your favourite TV programme or reading a magazine. This is just as important as all the other aspects of recovery, so don't skimp on it.

GROUP MEMBERS TALK ABOUT LIFE BALANCE

'You only get one life and you have to get out and live it – you might surprise yourself.'
ANDREA

'I don't find boredom is too much of a problem. I have to ensure at those times I don't get the "mischievous" bothersome thoughts.'
ANDREW

'I do get bored quite a lot of the time – I need to be challenged. I get anxious when I haven't enough to do.'
SARAH

16 Review – Lifestyle Changes

By now you will have realized that recovery from Anxiety takes a deal of work. But there is no need to be daunted. Remember to start small with each task and remember to be patient – it will take time for the changes to have an effect.

Summary of tasks so far

By now you should feel able to:

- keep an Anxiety diary
- score your Anxiety
- set goals
- do the simple breathing exercise.

By now you should have in place the following:

- relaxation every day
- exercise regularly, aiming for three times a week building to 20 minutes
- changes to diet where needed
- changes in caffeine consumption if needed
- changes to alcohol, nicotine and other drug consumption if needed
- a programme for better sleep if needed
- a programme to give more time for self if needed
- a programme for more challenges if needed.

Don't worry if you haven't managed all of these, because it does take time. The important thing is that you now understand what you need to do, and you have learnt not to be intimidated by the size of the task, because you know that small steps are best.

Dealing with difficult tasks

You may be finding any one of these tasks particularly difficult. If that is the case, take it more slowly and be prepared to work harder on it. It's quite likely that the task you find hardest is the one you most need to do, and the one that will bring you the most benefit when you succeed.

It's also possible that one or more of the tasks is difficult because it relates to your particular Anxiety. For instance:

Relaxation: you may be afraid of letting go.

Exercise: you may be afraid of fainting, or damaging your heart.

Food: you may be afraid of being sick or choking, or you may have an obsession with food hygiene.

Sleep: again you may be afraid of letting go, or you may be afraid of being more active.

More challenges: you may be afraid of taking on too much.

If you have this extra level of difficulty, then you will need to use the Anxiety-challenging skills that we will explore in the following chapters to enable you to complete your lifestyle changes.

It's important to understand the difference between a reluctance to make changes and an Anxiety-driven difficulty. For instance, if you feel that you can't make time for a recovery programme because your OCD is so time consuming, then your challenge is to find the time – even five minutes a day will help. However if your OCD is actually focused around one of the tasks then you will need to work on it as part of your main recovery programme rather than your lifestyle changes programme.

Use this space to write down your goals in each of the lifestyle areas.

RELAXATION

EXERCISE

DIET

CAFFEINE

ALCOHOL

NICOTINE

DRUGS

SLEEP

TIME FOR SELF

GROUP MEMBERS TALK ABOUT TAKING SMALL STEPS

'I get frustrated by the limitations imposed by my anxiety, but I'm learning to accept them. With tranquilliser withdrawal you have to let your body heal itself.'
ANDREA

'. . . even a thousand miles journey starts with just one small step.'
JULIE

'I had already mentally prepared myself by looking upon it as a set of stepping stones across a rapid moving stream, take it one step at a time, don't worry too much about the next step until you have successfully made a strong foothold on the one before it.'
NORMAN

Part Two

17 Taking the Next Step

Making changes to your lifestyle is only the beginning of your recovery from Anxiety – for some people there will be a huge impact on their Anxiety, although for others there will be very little difference. The only way to find out is to try – and in any case you will benefit from having a healthier lifestyle.

In this section we are going to move on to the next stage of constructing your recovery programme. Keep working on the lifestyle changes as you read through the next few chapters. Start by answering these questions.

1. Do you feel tense or worried all or most of the time? YES/NO

2. Do you have panic attacks? YES/NO

3. Are you afraid to go far from home? Or travel on public transport? YES/NO

4. Do you feel embarrassed in company, dread being the centre of attention, or dislike going to pubs or restaurants? Do you worry about blushing or trembling when speaking to people? YES/NO

5. Do you feel giddy when standing on the edge of a cliff? Or stifled in confined spaces like lifts or tunnels? YES/NO

6. Do you break out in a sweat at the thought of coming in contact with a spider? A mouse? Flying insects? A cat or a dog? Any other creature? YES/NO

7. Does the sight or thought of blood make you feel faint? Do you avoid

the dentist, or dread the thought of an injection? YES/NO

8. Do you feel compelled to wash yourself or your clothes, or clean your house, many times over? Do you have to check again and again that taps or lights are switched off, or doors locked? YES/NO

Look at the questions you answered with a yes. These will help you understand the nature of your Anxiety.

Yes to questions 1 and/or 2 are signs of Generalised Anxiety.
Yes to any of questions 3–7 indicates different types of phobia.
Yes to question 8 refers to OCD.

It is possible to have a combination of these. If your specific difficulty isn't mentioned, don't worry. The techniques we describe will still work for you.

Overview

We've already said that Anxiety affects every aspect of your being. Here is a brief overview:

-   **Physical**: whether or not you suffer from panic attacks, the effects of Anxiety always have a physical element. You may feel weak, faint or dizzy from shallow breathing. You may have headaches, neck, shoulder or back pain from muscle tension. Your digestion may be affected, with loss of appetite, dry mouth, nausea, swallowing difficulty. Bowels and bladder may be affected. Almost any part of your body can be affected by Anxiety.

-   **Emotional**: as well as the dominant emotion of fear you may also feel shame and lack of self-worth. You may also have underlying emotions, such as anger or grief, that you are not able to express openly.

- **Thinking**: your thoughts may race, be anxious or obsessive. You may be constantly saying negative things to yourself.

- **Behaviour**: you may avoid certain places or situations, or you may have to complete compulsive rituals

- **Whole self**: you may have poor self-esteem, fuelled by underlying beliefs about yourself. You may blame yourself for developing Anxiety.

- **Spiritual**: you may be dissatisfied with life, or feel that life has no meaning.

Effects of anxiety

Now examine each aspect of your life and decide how Anxiety affects it – use your notebook and work through each of the headings on the previous page. Here is an example from someone with severe agoraphobia:

Physical: sick and shaky, lightheaded.

Emotional: fear, even at the thought of going out, embarrassed when I have to tell people.

Thinking: supposing I do go out, and I collapse in public.

Behaviour: avoid going out, even to the dustbin.

Whole self: feel like giving up.

Spiritual: hate my life.

And another example from someone with OCD:

Physical: feel better doing rituals, apart from knot in stomach.

Emotional: fear, and ashamed of need to keep cleaning toilet.

Thinking: if I don't clean it'll be my fault if someone gets ill.

Behaviour: clean everything every day and clean toilet at least 10 times, more on bad days.

Whole self: hate myself.

Spiritual: I know that I'm responsible.

Understanding the detail of your particular Anxiety problem will help you focus on the changes you can make. As you change some things, you'll find that others change without you making a conscious effort. The lifestyle changes in section one were aimed at reducing some of the physical effects of Anxiety. This section will concentrate on your behaviour – the things that you do because of your Anxiety.

GROUP MEMBERS TALK ABOUT ANXIETY BEHAVIOURS

'I suppose you could say I'm a checker.'
ANDREW

'I thought if I stood up I would fall over and pass out. I phoned my partner and said I was feeling very strange but I didn't want to tell my mother I was ill.'
BRIDGET

'When my anxiety was very bad I didn't go outside my home at all, in fact I was confined to the bedroom, and to one side of the bed where I felt safe. Even going to the bathroom was difficult.'
JULIE

'I could not go out and even panicked when hanging the washing on the line. I was unsteady on my legs and would often feel as if I was going to fall through the ground. Turning my head or getting up from a sitting position made me dizzy and I would have to grab the nearest object to hang on to.'
MARGARET

> *'Wash those hands, check that light.*
> *Where's the energy to win the fight?*
> *Switch the light off, now put it back on.*
> *This O.C.D. has once again won.*
> *Oh no! My hands are dirty again.*
> *It's back to the sink and count up to Ten.'*

NORMAN

'I used to avoid everything.'
PEN

'At first I just used to avoid school assembly, then it was the pictures, and towards the end I wouldn't even go out in the back garden and put washing out.'
WENDY

18 Examining Anxiety Behaviours

There's no doubt that Anxiety does affect behaviour, although the details will be different for each person. Here are some of the most common Anxiety behaviours.

Escape

The urge to get out, get away, escape from the situation where the Anxiety or panic strikes can be overwhelming. It's part of the fight-or-flight mechanism which fills you full of physical energy and makes you want to *do* something. When you do leave, you find that you start to feel better quite quickly, so you'll tend to think that escaping makes Anxiety go away. Next time you'll feel even more keen to escape, and soon a pattern is established.

It's important to understand that escaping does not make Anxiety go away. The adrenalin surge of fight-or-flight always dies down, even if you stay put.

Avoidance

This usually follows on from escape. If getting out of a certain situation appears to make Anxiety go away, then it seems logical to avoid going into the situation in the first place. The problem with this is that pretty soon you've got a whole list of things that you can't do, life becomes a misery and you still suffer from Anxiety.

As well as avoiding places or situations you might also choose to avoid opening the paper or turning on the TV or radio in case there is an item about your phobic subject. You might avoid eye contact in social situations, or avoid using the phone or talking to people.

Avoidance is the main factor that keeps Anxiety going for agoraphobics, social phobics and people with panic attacks and single phobias. However it can also be an important factor for someone with OCD. If you know that using a public lavatory sets off a need to do rituals, then clearly you'll want to avoid public lavatories. This is also why someone with, say, a cleaning ritual might well end up doing no cleaning at all – better not to start in the first place.

The problem with avoidance is that it means you never test out your belief that you will be anxious if you enter the situation or engage with the behaviour.

Doing less

The physical symptoms of Anxiety can make you feel as if you are physically ill, in fact many people find it hard to believe that their problem is mental rather than physical. You can find yourself doing less and less because you feel so weak, tired and shaky. If you think that your panic attack is actually a heart attack, or that panic will damage your heart, you will retreat to the armchair and behave like an invalid. This is a vicious circle, because the less you do the worse you'll feel, physically, and the less you'll feel able to trust that your body will see you through the panic.

Safety behaviours

Nearly everyone with Anxiety has something they do that they believe keeps them safe. Someone with OCD with rituals, whether physical or mental, is doing that pretty well all the time. The trouble is the effect tends to wear off so that as time goes by you need to keep increasing the number or complexity of rituals to achieve the same feeling of safety.

People with other forms of Anxiety also have safety behaviours – always sitting by the door, always carrying your mobile phone, carrying spare

tranquillisers just in case, are good examples. Again these tend to
increase with time.

Effects of anxiety behaviours

There are two big problems with all of these behaviours.

1. As we've seen already, they tend to get worse with time, so that life
   becomes more and more restricted.

2. You believe that the behaviours are holding Anxiety in check, but in
   fact you never get to test that out.

Changing your behaviours will help you halt the increase and prove to
yourself that Anxiety does go down in the end whatever you do. All of
the behaviours have the same flaw, that is, they provide short-term relief
but overall Anxiety increases.

The aim is to change your behaviour very gradually, in small manageable
steps.

Exercise

Make a list of your Anxiety behaviours. Follow the four headings, and
add anything that you know you do even if it doesn't seem to fit any of
the headings.

ESCAPE

AVOIDANCE

DOING LESS

SAFETY BEHAVIOURS

OTHERS

GROUP MEMBERS TALK ABOUT SAFETY BEHAVIOURS

'The only situations I've ever really avoided are medical things.'
ANDREA

'Checking light switches/power sockets are off, doors are closed and locked, etc.'
ANDREW

'It was like I was almost out of my body. I kept thinking "I'm going to die on the number 16 bus". I phoned my mother who said "don't worry about me, get yourself to a doctor."'
BRIDGET

We had planned to be there early enough to strategically choose our seats, so that we (or rather I!) could easily "escape", should there be any need. At the time it sounded like a great idea but it meant a long unnerving wait before the start of the show.'
JULIE

'...often I had "jelly legs". If at all possible I preferred to tread on uneven ground because this made me concentrate on where I was putting my feet. Open areas of floor tiles, like you see in shopping malls, made me uneasy.'
MARGARET

> *But what if I need to use the loo?*
> *That would really put me in a stew.*
> *To touch the flush handle would be foul*
> *As I cover my hands with a thick clean towel.*
> *But it has to be a particular one.*
> *This isn't pleasant, it isn't fun.*

NORMAN

'Anything that upset me emotionally, even good things, brought on a panic attack.'
PEN

19 What Do You Want to Achieve?

You are beginning to have a clearer understanding of how your Anxiety problem affects your life. Perhaps you are realising that things aren't as bad as you thought, or perhaps you've had to face up to the full extent of your illness. This is painful but important – anything that you keep in the shadows of your mind is likely to turn into a bogeyman, scaring you because you don't understand it.

Now it's time to look at exactly what you want to achieve. You may say impatiently 'I just want to be alright' or 'I just want to be my old self again' but you need to be more specific than that.

No one is ever entirely anxiety free. Not only does everyday life produce anxiety (Will I find a parking space? Have I got time to dash into the bank?) but there is always the possibility of an unexpected difficulty (How am I going to cope with redundancy? How can I deal with my partner's anger?).

Anxiety is an essential part of life. It tells you when to be careful, and on the other side of the coin is your ability to feel excited about doing something new or challenging, such as starting a new job, or falling in love. You need both of those abilities.

The real problem is that your normal anxiety has mutated into an Anxiety condition, and it has taken control of your life. Wouldn't you like to wrest that control out of Anxiety's hands? Wouldn't you like to be in control again?

Remember the title of this book – *Free Yourself from Anxiety*. You have the power to do it, and you are the only one who can. However severely restricted you are, starting from where you are now, you can make improvements in your situation.

At first you may feel you aren't making any progress – but at least you will be preventing Anxiety from adding any more layers. And if you persevere, you will start to improve, however slowly. Finally, you will have learnt a set of lifetime skills that will keep you well, as long as you remember to use them.

Examining your responses

Let's look more closely at those impatient responses. Many people when they come for help will say:

- I want to get better
- I just want to be alright
- I just want to be my old self again
- I want to live a normal life
- I just want to be happy.

This is all perfectly understandable, but recovery doesn't come from aiming at this sort of goal. Remember, goals have to be SMART.

- *I want to get better* – this is too vague. Your goal must be Specific.

- *I just want to be alright* – can you define 'alright'? 'Alright' isn't Measurable.

- *I just want to be my old self again* – this is not Achievable, because every experience changes you, and so you will always be a different person from the one who fell into the black hole of Anxiety.

- *I want to live a normal life* – is this truly Relevant? Wouldn't it be better to live the life that's right for you?

- *I just want to be happy* – achieving happiness isn't Timeable. It can happen in an instant, or it can take years.

Instead you need to look for concrete, specific goals such as:

- I want to get back to work
- I want to have a relationship
- I want to travel abroad
- I want to go back to college.

Use your notebook to write down specific long-term goals for you. Don't let yourself become upset at the thought of how far off they seem. Instead, use the goals as your motivator. One day you will achieve them.

Be precise about your fears

Next, take one of your long-term goals and break it down further, looking at what is stopping you from achieving it right now. For instance, if your goal is to get back to work you might be stopped by:

- fear of having a panic attack at work
- fear of being with other people
- fears relating to the journey
- fear of a dirty environment
- fear of not having enough stamina to get through the day
- fear of being seen doing a ritual.

Your goals will be aimed at removing these fears from your mental agenda. They will be different for each person, because although there are broad categories of Anxiety disorder there are always differences of detail from person to person.

Cognitive Behaviour Therapy

We aim to show you how to achieve your goals using techniques based on Cognitive Behaviour Therapy (CBT). 'Cognitive' means 'relating to thoughts' – when you filled in the 'thinking' section in Chapter 17 you were describing your cognitive approach. 'Behaviour' means just that – how you behave.

The therapy aims to help you make changes to both your thoughts and your behaviours so that you can gradually release the grip that Anxiety has on you.

We are going to start with behaviour and move on to thinking in Part Three. This is because most people find it easier to change their behaviour, at first. Sometimes just changing behaviour is all a person needs to do, but most people find that they can get so far with it and then they come to a brick wall – that is when they need to move on to changing their thoughts.

You might say, why not go straight to changing thoughts then? The answer is that behaviour does have to be changed, and starting with thoughts is too challenging for most people. It's better to make some changes to your behaviour and enjoy the feelings of triumph that successes bring. This will help you to feel confident and motivated to work on your thoughts.

GROUP MEMBERS TALK ABOUT RECOVERY

'Keeping a diary was a great idea, because I felt obliged to tell the truth in it, and the only way I could record improvements in the diary was by doing the work and making the improvements.'
ANDREW

'...anxiety is not something that can be turned off like water from a tap.'
MARGARET

'My advice on recovery is to take it one step at a time and don't rush it. Start from wherever you're at and take the first step.'
WENDY

20 Looking at Change and Risk

We've already explained the key skills of relaxation, basic calm breathing and goal setting. Now we need to look at two more skills that relate to your mental attitude to recovery.

This is not the same as the cognitive part of CBT, which we'll deal with in Part Three. It's more about finding a mindset that will help your recovery rather than hinder it.

Anxiety has a very limiting effect on a person's life – they may avoid going out, restrict their social contacts, spend many hours on rituals instead of enjoying life, and so on.

There is a parallel effect on your mind. If you spend most of your time worrying, or working out how to avoid certain things, or how to manage life within the restrictions imposed by Anxiety, then you'll become mentally stale. Your thought processes will run along the same old grooves.

Then there is the fear factor. If even thinking about certain things brings a spurt of panic then you'll avoid thinking about them. You'll stop thinking of yourself as a person who can, for example, have a career, or travel the world, or face the challenges of life. You'll become self-protective and afraid to take on anything new in case it makes your Anxiety worse.

At the beginning of recovery work, people often give the impression that they want desperately to get better but they also want to hang on to their current mindset, even though this mindset is helping to maintain their

Anxiety. Changing your mindset is really important, but like everything else in your recovery programme, it can be done in small controlled steps. As you work through the exercises, you'll find that your mindset changes, slowly and gradually.

Key skill – accepting change

The first key skill is accepting that change is necessary. Change is scary for almost all of us. Just think of the first day at school, or the move to a new house. In fact if you look back at the Holmes-Rahe stress scale in Chapter 7 you'll see that almost everything on the list represents a change in status quo – someone was married, now they're divorced; were fit, now they're injured; were solvent, now they're in debt, and so on.

If you have experienced massive stressful changes, and have developed Anxiety as a result, it's no wonder that you don't want there to be any more change. Even if you haven't been through stress like this, the effect of Anxiety is to make you fearful of change. If you feel that you're only just coping with life as it is, you're bound to want things to stay the same, just in case you can't cope with anything new.

And yet everything about recovery involves a degree of change. If you were living off caffeine and thin air, you already know that you need to change your diet. If you were breathing badly, you're now learning to breathe well.

And because you've read this far, you know that the key is to make the changes in small controlled steps. You can get used to each step before you move on to the next one, and slowly but surely you will find yourself making the changes you need to make.

There will be more change as you work through this book. If you take it steadily you will manage it.

Finding the motivation for change

If change feels too challenging, and you aren't sure that you want to engage with it, then try this exercise.

In your notebook divide a page into four equal squares. Give each square a heading: Advantages of staying as I am, Disadvantages of staying as I am, Advantages of change, Disadvantages of change.

Next write down as many points as you can think of under each heading. Here's an example for someone with OCD around causing harm to others.

Advantages of staying as I am
I can be sure that I haven't hurt anyone as long as I do my checking rituals.

Disadvantages of staying as I am
I am isolated because of the time I spend checking.
My family life is disrupted.
I can't work so my income is low.
I'm very unhappy with my life.
My OCD is steadily getting worse.

Advantages of change
I could get back in touch with my friends.
My family would be much happier.
I'd be able to get back to work.
I might be happier.

Disadvantages of change.
I'd be very uncomfortable, I might not be able to bear it.
I'd feel like I was taking a huge risk, in case I did harm someone.

The key sentence here is 'My OCD is steadily getting worse'. This means that change is going to happen anyway, whatever you decide about undertaking a recovery programme. If you decide to do nothing, then the chances are that your Anxiety will get worse and you'll find yourself constantly fighting a rearguard action, trying to hold it back. On the other hand, if you take charge and work towards change that you choose, then you can make it happen in a positive way that leads you towards recovery.

Key skill – taking risks

Many Anxiety sufferers are naturally cautious people, or they learned caution from their families as they were growing up. Others become fearful of risk as a result of their experience of Anxiety.

When you read about the need for change, did you feel a stab of fear? Does it feel to you as if making changes is just too risky?

There is an element of risk involved in undertaking recovery work. You *may* have a panic attack if you venture out to the shops, you *may* feel worse rather than better if you cut down your rituals, you *may* embarrass yourself in public if you go out into the world.

But you know what we're going to say to you here – if you take it slowly, and break it down into small steps, then the risk at each stage is very small. If you persevere with the lifestyle changes and set yourself SMART goals, then you'll make the risk as tiny as possible.

But still, undertaking the programme will feel risky. The first time you step into the place you've been avoiding, the first time you walk away without finishing your ritual, will be challenging. At this point you need to ask yourself – do I want to carry on as I am, living in the black hole of Anxiety, or do I want to take a small, carefully structured risk as a step along the road to recovery?

Remember, nothing is without risk of some kind. You may feel that staying indoors or avoiding situations keeps you safe. But by placing such restrictions on yourself you *risk* losing friends, self-esteem, quality of life – quite a big trade-off for some short-term discomfort.

Learning to accept risk

This exercise will help you to assess risk objectively. In your notebook, divide a page into two columns, one headed Gains and one headed Losses. In the Gains column list all the benefits from taking the risk, and in the Losses column list every disadvantage of taking the risk.

Here is an example for someone with agoraphobia/social phobia who is trying to decide whether to go to a film with friends:

Gains
I'd like to see the film, I only see old films on TV now.
I could see my friends without having to make much conversation.
I know I'd feel better for getting out of the house.
I'd get a wonderful feeling of making progress with my recovery.

Losses
I might not enjoy the film.
I might feel too nervous to chat to my friends.
I might say or do something embarrassing.
I might feel so panicky that I can't go.
Something unforeseen might happen that I can't cope with.

Next, they look at the Losses list and decide whether they can manage the risks:

I might not enjoy the film – *I can cope with that.*
I might feel too nervous to chat to my friends – *they're used to me being quiet.*
I might say or do something embarrassing – *I can't bear the thought of that.*
I might feel so panicky that I can't go – *I can use relaxation to calm me.*
Something unforeseen might happen that I can't cope with – *my friends will look after me.*

Finally, they have to decide whether to take the risk. Clearly in this example they are most worried about embarrassment. They will have to decide whether to take this risk, or whether to aim for a smaller, more manageable goal.

GROUP MEMBERS TALK ABOUT THE RECOVERY PROCESS

'I've now come to realise that no magic wand or quick fix exists.'
NORMAN

'I'm very up and down, sometimes I feel I'll never get better. Other times, I know I am on the road to recovery.'
SARAH

'I am on a journey of self-discovery.'
TERESA

21 How Your Anxiety Affects Your Friends and Family

Many Anxiety sufferers have never told anyone about their problem. If you feel ashamed or embarrassed about having Anxiety you might feel quite unable to talk to anyone about it. You may also feel that you'll be labelled forever as someone who was mentally ill, that you won't receive any sympathy, or that you'll be forced to try treatments that you don't really want.

Even if you haven't told anyone, your friends and family are being affected by your illness. They may not know why you keep turning down invitations, or refuse to go on holiday with them, but they do know that something is preventing you.

People are naturally curious, and they'll wonder why you behave as you do. They may decide that you're just shy, or guess that there's some sort of problem. They may also come up with explanations that are way off beam – such as thinking you're unfriendly, or consider yourself too good to mix with them.

Did it upset you to read that? If only people knew what you're going through, then they'd have more sympathy, surely? Or would they judge you as weak, or pathetic? Struggling to keep your illness a secret adds greatly to the stress of Anxiety, so does worrying about who to tell, and how.

Only you can decide what is right for you, but many people have reported the great relief they felt when they finally confided in someone.

Telling someone about your anxiety problem

Many sufferers tell only one person, usually their partner or a family member. If they need a lot of support from that person they may then start to feel guilty about it, or perhaps resentful that the person isn't doing enough to help. It can make more sense to tell a few trusted people so that they can share the helping tasks. You may find that one person has a soothing presence and you enjoy their company, while another is helpful in a practical way.

It's important not to let your friends and family become part of the problem. If they always do your shopping for you, or check the house for spiders, or let you travel in the front seat of the car, then they are helping to maintain your Anxiety. No doubt they are busy people, and find it easier to go along with your immediate needs rather than take the time to help with recovery. With the best will in the world, they are doing exactly the wrong things. Of course temporary help, while you work on your recovery, is quite a different matter.

People with OCD do often admit to their difficulties, because they need help with their OCD. Sometimes they need help to complete their rituals, and sometimes they have a compulsive need to ask for reassurance. If you have OCD, you may have already involved your friends and family, even if it's just that they have to tolerate the extra time you need to do everyday tasks. They may also be obliged to live in a certain way (e.g. always wiping door handles after touching them) or may be involved in giving reassurance.

Whatever kind of help you have, you will at some point need to let go of it and take responsibility for yourself. Like every aspect of recovery, it can be planned as a series of goals aimed at gradually reducing your need for other people to support your Anxiety behaviour.

Carers

For a few people their Anxiety becomes so extreme that they need to be cared for by another person. This is a tough role and carers often become exhausted, while the person they are caring for has yet another worry – what happens if my carer can't carry on?

This is an extreme scenario of course, but it does give a tremendous motivation for undertaking recovery. Even someone whose Anxiety has become this bad can start a recovery programme – there is no situation so bad that it can't be turned round by slow steady repeated steps towards carefully chosen goals.

It's best to tell your carer what you are planning to do, so that you can work through the programme together. You may need to make changes in your daily routine, or ask for extra patience and understanding while you work on your goals.

GROUP MEMBERS TALK ABOUT SHARING AND ISOLATION

'Controlling my breathing as best as I could and gently encouraging myself, I staggered towards a payphone and called a friend for a bit of confidence boosting. As usual, my friend was wonderful ; the motivating words did the trick and I felt strong enough to continue.'
JULIE

'Looking back now, I am amazed at how I kept all the horrific thoughts and desperate feelings of self loathing to myself. The person I presented to family and friends could not do certain things because of anxiety and panic but the burden I was carrying within my head was far heavier and much more horrendous to me.'
MARGARET

22 Learning about Exposure Work

The basic tool that is used in CBT for changing behaviour is Exposure or systematic desensitisation. It is based on the understanding that Anxiety decreases the longer you tolerate it. This can be very hard to accept for someone who feels anxious all the time, or whose panics seem to last for ages, but the fact is that fight-or-flight is only designed as a short-term response to deal with immediate danger. Your body is very keen to switch off the fight-or-flight and with a little help from you, it will manage it.

In exposure work you choose to enter the situation that provokes your Anxiety in a controlled way. Someone with OCD will choose not to do their rituals, again in a controlled way.

There are some important aspects to exposure work that you need to understand before you get started.

- Start from where you are at.
- Set SMART goals.
- Structure the goals in small controlled steps.
- Repeat each step until you are comfortable with it.
- Do exposure frequently, at least once a day.
- Keep a record of each session, and score your Anxiety before, during and after the session.

Anyone with OCD whose obsessions and compulsions are both thought-based still needs to do exposure work, although they will need to design their programme around their compulsive thoughts rather than behaviours.

Working out an exposure plan

Continuing our example of someone who wants to get back to work, they have already looked at what is stopping them, and they know which form their Anxiety takes, so they know where to direct their efforts. The next stage is to look at intermediate goals that will take them towards the ultimate goal of returning to work.

- If they have a fear of having a panic attack, then they need to learn to be in situations that might provoke one.

- If they are afraid of other people, they need to practise being with other people.

- If they are afraid of travel, they need to practise travelling.

- If they have a fear of dirt, they need to practise being where there is dirt.

- If they have a fear of not getting through the day, they need to test their stamina.

- If they have a fear of doing their rituals in public, they need to cut down on their rituals.

It may be that you have more than one problem. An agoraphobic may have problems travelling, and being with other people. Someone with OCD may have problems with what they perceive as a dirty environment both while travelling and while at work.

The only answer is to take the issues one at a time, and the key at all levels of goal setting is to start with the one that you feel will cause you the least stress and be the easiest to achieve.

Listing your goals

Your next step is to make a list of five medium-term goals that will help you towards your main goal. Here's an example for an agoraphobic who wants to get back to work:

- Travel on the bus.
- Go to the corner shop and buy three things.
- Go to a coffee morning.
- Spend an hour in a busy shopping centre.
- Go away for a weekend.

Here's an example for someone with an obsession about dirt who wants to get back to work:

- Leave the house without cleaning toilet.
- Use public transport despite the dirt.
- Use a public lavatory.
- Reduce toilet cleaning to once a day.
- Use a lavatory in a pub.

Neither of these lists is in any particular order, because each individual will have their own ideas about what they might find easiest and hardest. It seems likely that the agoraphobic will find the weekend away the hardest to do, and either the bus journey or the corner shop the easiest. The person with OCD might find reducing toilet cleaning to once a day the hardest and the public lavatory the easiest. Or vice versa.

Make your own list of five goals in your notebook. Put the goals in order of difficulty. Remember to make your goals SMART.

There are some goals that fulfil all the SMART requirements that are still not very practical because of the need to keep repeating them. If you live in a village with only one bus a week, then you can't practise bus travel every day. If you are afraid of flying, you won't be able to get on a plane every day.

One answer is to look for other situations that imitate the one you fear. If you dislike being shut into a confined space with other people, then you can use lifts, cars, even meetings to practise that as well as getting on the bus or plane.

GROUP MEMBERS TALK ABOUT EXPOSURE FOR PANIC AND PHOBIAS

'I have done exposure work, on my own. You can do anything if you are prepared to put up with the discomfort.'
ANDREA

'Another thing I did was make a friend of my post box. I could see him from the window of my flat and he looked so friendly and solid. I called him Pat and it was 22 steps from my front door to get to him. Getting to Pat was my very first goal. My early exposure was all planned so that I could keep Pat in sight and it really helped me. I always greeted Pat when I passed him on my way out or on my return. I didn't feel silly about this, I knew it was helping me and I didn't have to tell anyone about it. Some time after I recovered I decided to move house, and it was quite a wrench to leave Pat behind.'
JULIE

'I've done exposure work on my own and with support. I still do it – I have a problem going beyond my comfort zone.'
PEN

'I tried exposure when I was 17, in hospital. I was scared of going outside, because I was afraid of meeting people from the past.'
SARAH

Exposure work for OCD

Doing exposure work for OCD is extremely effective, but it can be difficult to get started. If you feel in the grip of an eternal torment that is spiralling out of control, you may wonder how you can possibly start the process of fighting OCD.

OCD is caused by Anxiety. It is not a fundamental and unchangeable part of you. This can be difficult to accept when the thoughts seem so real and true. Like all Anxiety sufferers, your first steps in exposure work will be mainly a test, to see if it is really true that these awful feelings are caused by Anxiety and that Anxiety can go down. Gradually you will unlearn your automatic response to the trigger or triggers that set off your OCD.

Also you may feel that because of your obsessions you are odd or wicked. If you're feeling ashamed, guilty or terrified of going mad, you may try to cover up your problems. This increases your sense of isolation and adds to your stress, which only makes the OCD worse.

You have nothing to be ashamed or guilty about, and you are not going mad. It's as simple as that. OCD is an Anxiety disorder and it's not your fault that you have it. It's not a sign of weakness or moral degeneracy. It helps to talk to someone about this, and if you don't have someone you can confide in, then use a helpline or online service (see Appendix 2 for details). This will help you realise that there are many other people out there with OCD.

GROUP MEMBERS TALK ABOUT EXPOSURE FOR OCD

'I have done exposure work, when I was seeing a clinical psychologist. This was extremely helpful and I felt I could discuss any subject with her.'
ANDREW

'The therapist comes and says "how can I help?"
"It's this damn illness of mine!" you reply with a yelp.
They'll give exposure treatment to this bully you see.
Then this bully does nothing except run and flee.'
NORMAN

Exposure for panic attacks

A fear of having a panic attack is often the underlying fear behind the broad phobias such as agoraphobia, claustrophobia and social phobia. In other words, you tend to avoid certain situations because you are afraid of having a panic attack, not because of the situation itself. It is more unusual for someone with OCD to have a fear of having a panic attack, but it is a factor for some people.

When you start to do your exposure work your main concern will be to get through each stage without having a panic attack. This is understandable, and each time you manage it you will feel a little more confident. The trouble is, deep down, you will still be afraid of having another panic attack.

What you really need is to unlearn that fear – can you imagine how it would feel, if you could shrug and say 'let the panic come, it doesn't bother me?'

This leads to a two-pronged approach to exposure work for panic. You should follow the pattern of setting goals that are arranged with increasing difficulty, and you should start work on them in the hope that you won't have a panic attack while you're doing the easiest ones and building your confidence.

At some point though, you will start to work yourself a little harder, and then you might well have a panic attack. You will need to know how to cope – because you can cope, even though at the moment you think that you can't.

Coping with a panic attack

Usually when someone has a panic attack their instinct is to leave the situation they are in (the flight part of fight-or-flight). When the panic attack subsides, the person naturally feels that leaving the situation is the answer – when you leave, the panic stops. Except it was always going to stop whatever you did – fight-or-flight is a short term reaction remember.

So try to stay put if you possibly can. If you really must leave, try to calm yourself and return to the situation as soon as you can – within a few minutes if possible – and carry on with your goal.

Sometimes the reaction of the people around you makes the problem worse. If you are clearly in distress, and people try to help you it can add to the panic. Perhaps the first time you had a panic attack a helpful person called an ambulance, thinking you were having a heart attack. Probably you thought you were too. Even though it turned out that you weren't having a heart attack, the memory of that awful experience is still with you.

We would suggest that you start your exposure work with a helper, someone who understands and who can deal with kindly strangers who are concerned about you. Eventually you will set new goals that don't include a helper, but while you are building your confidence it's fine to have someone with you.

Breathing during panic attacks and exposure work

We've already explained that if you learn to control your breathing you can reduce your Anxiety. If you've been practising the breathing exercise in Part One you should now feel confident enough to use it to reduce Anxiety levels. Before you start an exposure session, steady yourself with calm slow breathing, counting in your head to make the Out breath longer than the In breath.

If you feel the first flutterings of panic at any time, use the calm breathing technique to dampen them down.

More about breathing

Now you can learn a little more about breathing. Sit comfortably, or lie down. Put one hand flat on your stomach, and the other on your chest, just below your neck. Sit quietly and feel how the hands move as you breathe. Which hand is moving the most? If it is the upper hand, the one on your chest, then you are breathing in a shallow way that isn't helpful for Anxiety.

It should be the lower hand that moves as you breathe, with the upper hand nearly still while you're at rest (it will move more when you're active) Here's an exercise to help you practise good breathing.

- Lie down flat on your back.

- Place your hands on your stomach with the fingertips just touching.

- Breathe through your nose.

- Breathe in and allow your stomach to expand like a balloon as you fill your lungs with air. Your fingertips will move apart as you do this.

- Breathe out and allow your stomach to shrink as you push the air out of your lungs. Your fingertips will move back together as you do this.

You can count in your head as you do this exercise. Once you've got the hang of it, try it sitting, and then standing. When you feel confident that you've mastered it, you can also use this kind of breathing during exposure sessions.

GROUP MEMBERS TALK ABOUT PANIC

'A little thought was dawning that this might be a panic attack – I never knew what people meant when they talked about panic, I thought it was what you felt if, say, a car swerved towards you.'
BRIDGET

*'. . . at the Eurostar terminus, that **Huge** open space by a very steep escalator proved to be too much for me and Anxiety started to play havoc with my nerves, flooding me with negative thoughts. I then was very close to panicking and giving up.'*
JULIE

23 Planning Your Exposure

The next stage is to take the easiest one of your goals and plan how you will achieve it. It may be that the lifestyle changes you have already made have created enough improvement that you feel able to tackle the goal straight away. By all means try it, but don't push yourself too hard.

Probably you will feel that the goal is beyond you, in which case you can break it down into a series of smaller goals. Remember to make each one SMART, and remember that you need to be able to repeat it. Use your notebook to write down the goal, and the steps that you will take to achieve it.

Exposure ladders

Working through your goals is like climbing a ladder, where each rung takes you closer to your ultimate goal at the top of the ladder. When you first write out the steps you may feel that you will never reach the top of the ladder – it's out of sight, lost in the clouds. Never mind. Write out the steps anyway, and start climbing the first few rungs. Don't think too much about the higher rungs – eventually they will come into sight and you will be able to tackle them.

Do bear in mind that you need to feel some Anxiety while you are doing your exposure. If you don't feel any, you won't have learnt anything, and if you feel too much you'll feel disheartened. In practice, most people will need to do many repetitions of the first few steps while they are regaining their confidence, and they may have to do fewer repetitions as they get further up the ladder.

Visualisation

If you can't see a way on to the ladder, then start with visualisation. Lie or sit comfortably, close your eyes, and imagine yourself doing the goal. Try to create a complete picture, including not only a visual picture of the event, but also the noises and other sensations associated with it. Put yourself in the picture behaving calmly and succeeding at the goal.

The examples that follow give you an idea of how to create your ladder.

Panic ladder

Here's an exposure ladder for someone who had a panic attack in a busy supermarket and now dreads going back there in case it happens again. Their ultimate goal is to return to the supermarket and they devise the following steps:

Visit corner shop when quiet.
Visit corner shop when busy.
Visit shopping precinct and walk past supermarket late in the day, when deserted.
Visit supermarket at quiet time, with a helper, and buy one item.
Visit supermarket at quiet time, without helper, and buy one item.
Visit supermarket at quiet time, with a helper and buy several items.
Visit supermarket at quiet time, without helper, and buy several items.
Visit supermarket at busier time, with a helper, and buy one item, and so on.

Agoraphobia ladder

Let's look at someone who's housebound and who feels there's no point in trying any more. In fact the tiniest goals can lead to bigger things – it's always worth trying, however silly or ridiculous it might seem to do these things.

Visualise leaving house.

Put on coat and outdoor shoes (to get used to the feel of them again).

Put on coat and outdoor shoes, stand by front door till Anxiety subsides.

Put on coat and shoes, take rubbish to dustbin.

Walk to first lamppost, return home.

Walk to second lamppost, return home.

Walk to postbox, post letter.

Eventually someone with agoraphobia needs to practise staying in situations, so they could move on to the shopping ladder in the panic example, or they could devise a new ladder that focuses on being with other people.

Specific phobia ladder

If you have a specific phobia, exposure is designed to increase your tolerance of the thing you fear. Each ladder has to be individually tailored. Here is an example for someone with spider phobia.

Look at a cartoon of a spider.

Look at a photo of a spider.

Touch the photo of a spider.

Watch a video about a spider.

Look at a spider in a sealed jar.

Hold a jar with a spider in it.

Hold a spider.

Sometimes it can be difficult to repeat the exposure – thunderstorms for instance only occur occasionally. Consider buying a CD or DVD of the thing you fear and using that in your ladder.

Generalised Anxiety Disorder ladder

If you have GAD, exposure work can be used to increase your activity level and build up your stamina. Goals might include meeting friends, going to public places, doing voluntary work or doing a sport or social activity. Construct a separate exposure ladder for each one.

There is another aspect to GAD which is the act of worrying itself. If your attempts to do more are constantly interrupted by worry, you can create an exposure ladder to help you reduce the time you spend worrying. Start by writing down your worries in your notebook – this will help you see them more objectively. You can set goals that aim to cut down the number of thoughts, or reduce how many times you allow yourself to go round the thinking loop. Another approach is to set aside times for worrying:

Worrying allowed on the hour, every hour, for ten minutes.
Reduce each session to five minutes.
Omit every other session, and so on.

Travel phobia ladders

Fear of travelling often forms part of a wider group of phobias which make up the agoraphobia cluster, or may apply to a specific situation such as driving on motorways. Here are two examples.

Travelling by bus

Take the bus for one stop, at a quiet time, sitting near the door with helper beside you.
Repeat, but for two stops.
Take the bus for five stops, sitting apart from helper.
Take the bus for one stop with helper following by car.
Take the bus for two to five stops with helper following by car.
Take the bus one stop without helper following.
Take the bus two to five stops without helper following.
Repeat the journey at a busier time.
Practise taking the bus to visit friends, go shopping etc.

Travelling by car

Be a passenger with helper driving:

Sit in the stationary car for a short time in passenger seat with helper in driving seat.
Go for a five-minute drive on quiet street with helper driving.
Go for a longer drive in quiet area with helper driving.
Go for a longer drive in traffic with helper driving.
Go for a longer drive including dual carriage way with helper driving.
Go for a longer drive including motorway with helper driving.

If you need to re-establish yourself as a car driver, then consider repeating the steps above with a helper in the passenger seat, then following you in another car. However if you feel you won't be safe on the road, for whatever reason, then consider taking refresher driving lessons.

Social phobia ladder

This example is for someone whose social phobia is around eating and drinking in front of other people.

Invite someone into your home for a short visit.
Have a slightly longer visit, make a drink but don't drink yours.
Have a visit where they are able to watch you make the drink.
Have a visit where you also drink something.
Walk past a fast food outlet, observe people eating and drinking.
Accompany someone to a fast food outlet but don't eat or drink yourself.
Accompany someone to a fast food outlet, eat or drink something yourself.
Continue the process to include pub meals, and then restaurant meals.

An exposure ladder can be constructed for any Anxiety disorder. If you still feel stumped about how to construct your own ladder, then there are many leaflets available from No Panic or First Steps to Freedom.

GROUP MEMBERS TALK ABOUT EXPOSURE

'The thing that helped me the most was taking the time to visualise the exposure before I did it. I used to rehearse it mentally, taking it step by step and always visualising a successful outcome.'
JULIE

'What he [the therapist] *did recommend was that it was imperative to keep to a maintenance programme by practising the exercises I had been taught.'*
NORMAN

24 Exposure for OCD

For someone with OCD, exposure work focuses on the element of compulsion and its companion, avoidance. (Obsessions are dealt with in the cognitive part of CBT – see Part Three.)

It can seem as if OCD recovery requires the opposite of other Anxiety disorders. A person with, say, social phobia, has to find a way to stay in social situations – they have to do something they *don't* want to do. A person with OCD has to find a way to stop doing their compulsions – they have to stop doing something they *do* want to do.

In fact the underlying problem is the same – learning to tolerate Anxiety until it dies down and eventually goes away. The person with social phobia will feel anxious if they are in a social situation. The person with OCD will feel anxious if they don't do their compulsions. Both can gradually learn to put up with the anxious feelings until they start to go down.

Understanding compulsions
There are often two elements to compulsions:

1. Having to do the compulsion a certain number of times, or until it feels like enough times.

2. Having to do the compulsion in a certain way – if a mistake is made, you have to go back to the beginning, and the one with the mistake doesn't count.

Both elements can be tackled with exposure work. Start by asking yourself two questions:

1. What do I do because of my fears?
2. What have I stopped doing as a consequence of my fears?

Answering both questions might produce two quite long lists, for instance:

1. Because of my fears of contamination I wash myself several times a day all over, I clean my kitchen and bathroom every day, I wipe over all shopping that comes into the house with disinfectant and I have to decontaminate myself if I've been out of the house.
2. As a consequence I've stopped growing my hair because short hair is easier to wash, stopped cooking meals from scratch because of having to keep my kitchen clean, stopped buying fresh fruit and vegetables because they can't be disinfected and stopped going out much as it takes so long to decontaminate myself afterwards.

Put the lists in order of difficulty and choose whichever item seems easiest for your first goal. Remember that your goals need to combine two elements:

1. doing something you have been avoiding (exposure); and
2. stopping yourself from doing the compulsive rituals (response prevention).

'Response prevention' is a technical term used in clinical treatment for OCD but it doesn't mean you have to stop completely all at once. Like all exposure work, you are more likely to succeed by approaching it gradually, step by step. You can start by cutting down on the number of times you repeat a compulsion, or by increasing the time between exposure and starting the ritual. See the examples below.

Example: compulsive hand washing

Reduce the number of washes by one, maintain that until comfortable, then reduce by one more and so on.

OR

Delay time of starting to wash by one minute, delay time of starting to wash by two minutes, and so on.

If your OCD makes you very slow at everyday tasks try setting a time limit – start with a generous time and reduce it day by day. It can help to have someone else show you how they complete the task within a normal timescale, but don't ask them to show you every time, just once.

If your OCD includes asking for reassurance, then the people you ask will need to be involved in your exposure work. Ask them to limit the number of times they give reassurance to you.

OCD with compulsive thoughts

Everyone knows you can't stop yourself thinking just like that. If someone says to you 'don't think about a yellow car with red spots' you will immediately get an image of a car like that in your mind. So don't waste energy trying to simply stop yourself from having compulsive thoughts. Instead look for ways of reducing the amount of time you spend with them, or reducing the number of times you need to do them. You can look at ways of resisting the compulsion for instance:

- Thought stopping: say, or think, the word STOP.

- Thought switching: deliberately start to think about something else – choose this in advance, and choose something you find pleasant.

- Distraction techniques. These are explained in Chapter 26.

If you consider that this kind of technique makes matters worse because it gives the thought too much importance, then try ways of reducing the importance:

- Expose yourself to the trigger for the thought until you are tired of it.

- Exaggerate the thought until it becomes ridiculous.

- Practise letting go of the importance of the obsession – see it as background noise that can be ignored.

Examine your behaviour while you are busy with your thoughts (this is known as ruminating). Do you stop what you are doing so that you can sink into your ruminations? Simple tasks, or distractions such as listening to the radio, might help you come out of yourself. Or set aside a fixed time each day when you are allowed to brood.

Choose a behaviour that you can train yourself to associate with letting go of the thoughts – something as simple as standing up and leaving the room every time they start.

If your OCD includes strong mental images you can take control by pretending you are filming the image – you can reduce the size of the worrying part (dog faeces for instance) or you can zoom in on something harmless at the edge of the picture such as a patch of grass.

GROUP MEMBERS TALK ABOUT OBSESSIONS AND COMPULSIONS

'Without warning a voice, seemingly from nowhere, said "Kill him."...I became very hot and waves of panic washed over me. I could not get the words out of my mind. I was frantic with fear at this terrible thought...I thought I must be losing my sanity, what other explanation was there?'
MARGARET

'I had to kneel at one of the graves and rub my hands in the dirt amongst the gravestone,...I have since learnt that this type of treatment is called exposure therapy where your fears are faced head on. I had already mentioned to the staff that I had this fear of anything related to death, and that afternoon was certainly spent facing this problem head on. My anxiety level was able to be kept under control for most of that time, and on arrival back at the hospital I was prevented from washing my hands which I feel did me some good.'
NORMAN

25 Working with a Helper

It can be a good idea to enlist the help of someone you trust while you're doing exposure work – the return-to-the-supermarket ladder in Chapter 23 included using a helper. Of course it isn't essential and many people complete their recovery with very little help.

If you are going to ask someone to help you with your exposure, you both need to understand certain things.

- You are in control of your recovery. If you are attempting a goal, you will explain it to them, and explain how you would like them to help. You can also decide how you want them to behave if you decide to abandon the goal. We suggest that you ask them to talk to you calmly, to ask you if you feel you can go on just a little longer, and if you can't, then they accept that the goal will stop there.

- They must never trick you, because you have to be able to trust them absolutely. So no promising you that it will only be a short drive, and then taking you further, or coaxing you out of the bathroom and then refusing to let you back in.

- They need to be able to stay calm when you are anxious. It won't help you if they become panicky in response to your distress.

- They don't need to understand the nature of Anxiety disorders, as long as they can accept that you need to do exposure in a certain way.

- They must never belittle your difficulties.

- They must give you their time and attention – it's no use at all if the helper on the supermarket ladder thinks they are going to do their own shopping at the same time.

- You must understand that your helper isn't a saint – just someone who is trying to do their best for you.

- And finally, don't feel guilty about asking for help. When you are better, you'll find a way to repay them for their kindness.

Arranging help with panic and phobia exposure

Talk to your helper before you start the exposure session. Explain exactly what you hope to achieve with the goal and what you want the helper to do. Their overall function is to help you feel safe in a frightening situation. They will do this just by being there, and also there are things they can say to help:

- Grounding – remarks that remind you what to do such as 'just breathe out slowly'.

- Reassurance – simple phrases such as 'you can do this' or 'take your time'.

- Distraction – helping you to focus on something outside your fear, to remind you that the outside world is still there, for instance 'that girl's got nice hair' or 'did I tell you we're going to paint the kitchen?'.

- Perspective – remarks that remind you this won't last for ever such as 'we'll have a cup of tea when we get home' or 'mustn't miss EastEnders tonight'.

- Praise – sharing in your jubilation when you achieve a goal, however small it may be.

Explain to them that you might not give very coherent answers to their remarks, and that this doesn't matter.

Arranging help with OCD exposure

If you haven't involved anybody else in your OCD you can still choose to ask for help with exposure. Explain to the helper what your goal is, and what they can do to help you.

Stopping rituals and compulsive thoughts

Your helper can use the same techniques described above for helping with panic and phobias:

- Grounding – remarks that remind you what to do such as 'just breathe out slowly' or 'you were going to stop after ten minutes.'

- Reassurance – simple phrases such as 'you can do this'.

- Distraction – taking your mind away from your obsession, remarks such as 'Did you see that goal on Match of the Day?' or 'I really must get some new shoes.'

- Perspective – remarks that remind you this won't last for ever such as 'let's have a hot drink in a while' or 'pizza for dinner tonight, can't wait.'

- Praise – sharing in your jubilation when you achieve a goal, however small it may be.

Asking for reassurance

Your helper needs a special technique if you tend to ask repeatedly for reassurance that something is alright, or is done. Agree with them beforehand that they will only reply once, and that after that they will say something like 'we agreed that I wouldn't give you any more reassurance.' It's best if they stick with just one answer, whatever you say. If you become distressed, they can comfort you, but they can't give reassurance. It's important that they stay calm, and keep their voice calm.

GROUP MEMBERS TALK ABOUT WORKING TOWARDS RECOVERY

'The trigger for my recovery was when I suddenly had to fly to get to an important family occasion. I had been comfortable with my agoraphobia and had made friends with it, so when I realised I had to travel and go on a plane, outside my comfort zone, my anxiety went through the roof. I did manage to get there, with a lot of help, and afterwards I started on recovery work.'
JULIE

'You no longer need to keep asking for reassurance. However, how will loved ones cope with this change when they've developed the habit of constantly giving in to your demands for reassurance? This is one of the things you may wish to discuss with them, and remind them that it's not particularly helpful to keep giving this reassurance.'
NORMAN

'I did some one-to-one work with a co-worker at first, then a couple of us would go out together and we would talk to take the focus away from feeling scared. I began walking round the car park, then gradually built up over 6 months until I could go into town. I can go out now on my own, ... I still feel anxious but now I am no longer enormously afraid .'
SARAH

'I've done exposure. I asked the doctor and he organised a carer to take me out twice a week for 3 hours at a time. I've been places I never thought I'd go – I went to Old Trafford to see the flowers for the Munich memorial.'
WENDY

26 Exposure – Coping Skills

When you first start on exposure work it can be helpful to adopt a range of coping skills. These are little crutches that help you through the challenges, and that you know you will eventually do without. They are very similar to safety behaviours (Chapter 18) but they are aimed at helping you get through your goals and you will drop them as soon as you can.

We have some suggestions for coping skills that have worked well for other people over the years, but anything that works for you is fine. There are only two considerations:

1. It mustn't be damaging (such as using alcohol to get through).

2. It mustn't feed into your Anxiety (such as saying a prayer if you have compulsive thoughts around prayer).

Read through the list and pick out anything that appeals to you. If you think that panic will cause the skills to fly out of your head, write your chosen ones on a little card to carry with you.

Your body

- **Breathing** – if you've been practising slow calm breathing you'll now reap the benefit as you'll be able to use it to keep yourself calm during your exposure sessions.

- **Paper bag** – people who suffer from panic sometimes find it helpful to carry a paper bag (never a plastic one and not too small or too large). At the onset of panic, breathe out into the bag, then breathe in from the bag. Do this for a few breaths. It calms you because you are breathing back in your old air, instead of sucking in fresh air that will give you too much oxygen. Breathing into and out of your cupped hands has a similar effect.

- **Exercise** – if your exercise programme is going well you can remind yourself how fit you now are, and that your body can clearly cope with Anxiety. This is specially useful if panic makes your legs turn to jelly – if you are fit, you can be sure that they will carry you, however shaky they feel.

Your helper

If your helper has read Chapter 25 they already understand what they can do to help you. In addition they can remind you to use your coping skills.

Mental distractions

- **Counting** – choose something to count – red cars, lampposts, people with hats on – to take your mind off the anxious feelings.

- **Mental arithmetic** – start from 100 and count backwards in 7s, or multiply numbers together.

- **Reciting –** repeat your favourite poem, hymn or prayer in your head. Or try the words of a song, and walk along to the rhythm of it.

Physical distractions

Carry something that will distract you, and help you stay focused on the goal rather than the Anxiety, e.g.:

- **Something interesting** in your pocket that you can touch for reassurance: a pebble or coin, your keys.

- **Sweets –** many people find it helpful to suck a strong mint.

Relaxation

If you've been faithfully doing relaxation at least once a day, you'll now find that your mind and body will be conditioned to relax when you hear the words on the recording. You can:

- **Play** the recording through a headset while you're doing exposure.

- **Repeat** to yourself your favourite phrase from the recording.

- **Picture** your favourite scene from a visualisation recording.

Emotions

- **Anger** – surprisingly, anger is helpful for some people. Anger gives us energy, and you can use that energy to drive yourself through a difficult exposure session. It's best if it comes naturally though, arising from the frustration you feel. Don't deliberately wind yourself up to anger.

- **Delight** – think of the joy you'll feel when you manage your goal, or focus on the pleasure your success will bring to the people who care about you.

Thoughts

Imagine feeding your anxious thoughts into a shredder, or tie them to a balloon and let them float away.

Plan an escape route

When you're planning your exposure, it's okay to work out how you'll escape if you need to. There is so much embarrassment surrounding Anxiety, and so many people dread humiliating themselves in public, that it's worth working out what you'll do if you need to get out. Something as simple as patting your pocket, or looking in your bag, tells any onlooker that you've forgotten something and explains why you've turned back.

Reward system

Finally, create a reward system for yourself. When you're planning an exposure session always think about how you will reward yourself when it's all over. Because you need to do exposure every day, most rewards will be small treats that are easy to arrange and not too expensive. Every now and then you can give yourself something bigger, or more costly. Having something to look forward to will help keep you motivated, and improve the quality of your life.

Just like coping skills, rewards can be anything as long as they are not:

1. harmful to you

2. part of your Anxiety.

Rewards can also be incorporated into the exposure work, so that you may set yourself the task of going out to buy your favourite magazine, or use the time freed up by not doing rituals to watch TV.

Here are some suggestions:

- Take a hot relaxing bath.

- Watch your favourite TV programme, video or DVD.

- Eat a cream cake or chocolate – yes, you can break the diet rules occasionally!

- Cook your favourite meal.

- Read a book or your favourite magazine.

- Phone someone you rarely talk to.

- Enjoy the garden, if you have one.

GROUP MEMBERS TALK ABOUT COPING SKILLS

'My coping skills are positive self-talk and I believe that you can achieve most things if you'll tolerate the discomfort.'
ANDREA

'As for coping skills, when I trained in hypnotherapy I was very drawn to the idea of a gentle touch on the right earlobe to remind you to be calm, but I have to say it's never worked for me!'
ANDREW

'My most important coping skills are breathing and visualisation. I used to use physical props such as a bottle of water or some ice cubes at home, mints, boiled sweets and a little hard ball to squeeze and relieve my tension. I gave them all up gradually. The mints were the last to go as I used to get a very dry mouth (I had sugar-free mints so that I didn't get a sugar rush).'
JULIE

'My main coping skills are relaxation, and meditation, which stops the internal chatter.'
PEN

'My coping skills are: controlling my breathing, regular exercise, music (I put on headphones and block out anxious thoughts), making myself socialize even when I feel I can't be bothered and asking for support from friends.'
SARAH

'My main coping skill was using my bike – you can always escape and come back quicker.'
WENDY

27 Exposure – Your First Goal

After reading this section you should understand how to do exposure work to change your Anxiety driven behaviour in small, manageable steps. You have established your long-term goals, and your medium-term goals, and broken one of those down into a series of small, repeatable steps, like a ladder.

You know that recovery entails accepting change and facing risks in a controlled way. You know that you need to feel some Anxiety while doing exposure, but not enough to overwhelm you.

You've thought about how the people around you are involved in your Anxiety, and affected by it, and you've decided whether to use a helper during your exposure sessions.

Use your notebook to keep records of your exposure work, scoring your Anxiety on a scale of 0–10.

You've learnt a little more about healthy breathing. You know about coping skills and you've put a reward system in place. Use the checklist below to make sure you have everything ready, and then start your exposure work.

CHECKLIST

Long term goal(s):

Five medium-term goals in order of difficulty: 1.

2.

3.

4.

5.

Ladder leading to easiest medium term goal:

Helper YES/NO

Coping skills:

Reward system:

JULIE'S EXPOSURE – PHOBIA

'I had a phobia of thunderstorms and especially the noise they make which started when I was very young, after a bad experience. I had reached a point where I could travel to my family in France but I never went in the summer, because they live in the mountains where they have spectacular thunderstorms at night in hot summers. I missed all the family get togethers that were always in the summer. I started work in February, to be ready to travel in July. In England we don't have many thunder-storms so I got a tape of a thunderstorm from First Steps to Freedom.

I couldn't listen to it, even looking at it terrified me. Playing the tape became a goal. I tried visualising myself playing the tape and being calm, but for once this didn't work for me. I asked my mentor to be on the phone while I listened to the tape. The first time we were on the phone for 3 hours. First he talked me through relaxation, then I pressed play and let the tape run at very very low volume while he kept talking to me. Slowly I put the volume up. I was getting more and more agitated but we did get the volume very high and the thunder sounded very real – this triggered a massive panic attack and we had to stop. We had sessions twice a week for three weeks until I could tolerate the tape at full volume for 10 minutes.

The next stage was for me to listen to the tape on my own, knowing that I could phone him. At first I could only take three or four minutes but I gradually got it up to the full 20 minutes. I kept it loud so we had to shout but I did learn to stay with the situation. After a month I could listen to the whole tape without phoning him.

The next stage was to recreate lightning. I got three friends to come round with their cameras. We made the room dark and they took flash photos while a fourth friend managed the tape, so that after every flash I heard a peal of thunder. At first I had to call my mentor on the phone to get through it – we did it about four times before I was OK. The flashes didn't frighten me as much as the noise.

After that we tried it at night, outside in the rain, with the tape player the cameras, and my mobile phone. We did it a few times and I could cope without phoning. I repeated the exposure once a week till I went to France in July and there was only one small thunderstorm.'

ANDREW'S EXPOSURE – OCD

'My therapist gave me a notebook in which she'd already put the headings: Time, Date, Situation, Ritual, Alarm level beforehand, Time Spent or Number of Repetitions, Alarm level afterwards and Thoughts.

One of my rituals was when I was leaving the house, looking at the door whilst locking it, checking it was closed, and feeling anxiety that it really was closed. 8 is a comfort number for me so I used to check it 2 by 8 times, and I had to go through the count without blinking. Once I started recording it over the next few days it got much worse and I was up to checking 8 by 8 times. I saw the therapist again and I felt raw and angry from having to open myself up so much and show her the notebook. However by discussing it with me she was able to put a more logical slant on it.

After two or three weeks I realised it was decreasing – I wanted to reduce it in the notebook and I didn't want to cheat, it had to be real. It was like I was in a play and I had to play the part well. I also tried to make my thoughts more positive so that I could write down more positive thoughts.

It was difficult to put my feelings into words and that sent my anxiety up. Once I started to reduce it I was cautious about admitting I was doing well – if you're successful then you're running the risk of a setback, and there's a feeling that you're not worthy of success.

The turning point came when I realised that the therapist had the confidence that I would make progress. I made really good improvement, I could still improve but the vast majority of the time it isn't a problem and I can live my life quite comfortably.'

28 Plateaux and Setbacks

When you set up a recovery programme you aim to work steadily, curbing your impatience and taking one step at a time. And yet recovering from Anxiety is not a smooth, steady process. You will have good days and bad days, times when anything seems possible and times when nothing goes right.

Everybody's recovery moves at a different pace, and to a different rhythm. You may start wonderfully, going off like a rocket, and then grind to a halt. You may find it impossible to get started and feel quite despairing, and then suddenly everything falls into place. Some goals may take weeks to crack, others you may manage on the first attempt.

Whatever your particular experience, you can be as sure as eggs are eggs, there will be difficulties at some point, so you might as well have an understanding of how to deal with them.

Whatever you do, don't give up. Don't let yourself slide back into the hopeless black hole. You've started to work towards recovery and however tough things get, you can find a way to keep going.

Plateaux
A plateau occurs when you've had some success with exposure, but then reach a point when you don't seem to be able to get any further.

Setbacks
Setbacks are bound to be more worrying, but virtually everybody has

them. Think of anything else you've undertaken and you'll see that it's inevitable – whether you were trying to play the piano, make cakes, get qualified or fit a new kitchen there were bound to be times when you felt like you were going backwards.

It is much more realistic to expect setbacks and plan for them, rather than assume that your recovery is going to go without a hitch or two along the way. That way, you will be prepared for them and have more confidence that you can stay on the ladder, even if you have to take a step or two back.

Dealing with plateaux and setbacks
For both plateaux and setbacks there are various things you can try:

Take a break
Did you attempt too much and tire yourself? Is it time to take a break? If you suspect that you simply need some time out from recovery work, then by all means take it. Give yourself a week without attempting any new goals. Use the time to repeat well-established goals, and to look after yourself with good diet, rest and exercise. When you are ready to start work on your recovery again, take it a little more slowly.

Review your diary
Remind yourself how far you've come by reading your diary from the beginning. You'll almost certainly have forgotten how bad things were, and how much progress you have made. Take note of any other problems you've had, and how you overcame them. When you read the pages that record a setback, don't despair. Instead try to work out if there were any special circumstances that might have caused the setback.

Talk to someone who understands
If you've been part of a local recovery group, or a telephone group, make contact with someone you met on the group and talk it through with

them. Or phone one of the helplines and talk it through with a volunteer. They speak to hundreds of people every week and they know how common plateaux and setbacks are. They also know that both can be overcome.

Reassess your goals

Have you set two of the rungs on the ladder too far apart, and is that why your progress has stalled? Can you see a way of putting another step in between? Or did you try to take too big a step, and instead of moving up, you lost your footing and slipped back down?

Lateral thinking

Look at the ladder you are currently working on and see if you can climb it a different way. For instance, someone who couldn't progress with their dental phobia because of the long gaps between appointments volunteered as a driver for elderly people – the regular visits to the surgery helped them to be much more relaxed there. Someone who suffered a setback when reducing the number of times they checked their cooker changed to the goal of restricting the amount of time they spent checking – later they were able to return to the original goal.

Above all, don't give up. It may be that exposure work has taken you as far as it can. Maybe it's time to start cognitive work.

GROUP MEMBERS TALK ABOUT PLATEAUX AND SETBACKS

'You ... ought to take the approach that a setback is a sign that you are getting better and learn from it to move forwards again. After all, you pulled through it before so there is no reason why you shouldn't pull through it again this time.'
JULIE

'Your physical and mental abilities are not damaged by your anxiety illness and you will always be capable of coping with an emergency.'
MARGARET

'I feel like I was living in a different world to everyone else. It frustrates me to see other people making the same mistakes I did.'
TERESA

Part Three

29 Anxiety on Trial

Picture a scene at the Old Bailey. Look, in the dock there's Anxiety, there's the judge, wearing a wig, and an interested crowd in the public seats. What does your Anxiety look like? Male or female? Big or small? Defiant or cowering? Blustering bully, or evil shadow?

Anyway, here come the witnesses for the prosecution.

'Anxiety stopped me going to my best friend's wedding.'
'Anxiety made me wash my hands till the skin was red raw.'
'Anxiety kept me on the couch day after day.'
'Anxiety made me helpless and hopeless.'
'Anxiety ruined my life.'

The judge looks stern. What can Anxiety possibly say in defence?

'Your Honour, I only did it to keep them safe, and they wanted to be safe, didn't they? Yes I did keep them at home, or in one room even, and I did stop them doing all sorts of things and I did make them do other things, but supposing something dreadful had happened? What if that wedding was a nightmare of panic and they ruined it by rushing out of the church in the middle of the ceremony? Supposing those hands had germs on them and someone got sick and it was all their fault for not washing their hands enough? And if you feel so tired and weak, isn't the couch the best place to be? Oh Your Honour, I didn't ruin their lives, life is so full of danger and woe and all sorts of terrible things, I only did my best to keep them safe and if I may say so Your Honour, you're looking a bit peaky, maybe you'd better go for a lie down, it wouldn't do to pass out in the middle of the court now would it?'

The prosecution lawyer isn't having any of it. He, or she, points a stern finger at Anxiety.

'You did all these things for your own malicious purposes. You enjoy the power it gives you over these innocent people. I ask the jury to return a verdict of GUILTY!'

GROUP MEMBERS TALK

'Anxiety, that familiar and much dreaded Bully, played havoc with my nerves all day, reminding me of how hard everything used to be.'
JULIE

'A reference on television, radio or an article in a newspaper about a person being deliberately injured or killed would send me into a nightmare of conjecture. Simple tasks like helping put on a school tie would trigger off my imaginings of strangulation and panic would engulf my whole being.'
MARGARET

30 Let the Trial Commence

In this section, we are going to put your Anxiety on trial. Because it lives inside your head it can be difficult to examine it as if it were a separate entity, but that is what cognitive work is all about.

We are going to examine the ways Anxiety works inside your mind and affects your thought processes. Take your time reading this section, it contains a lot of ideas and you'll want to get your head round each one before you do the exercises that relate to it. And while you're working through this section, remember to press on with your lifestyle changes from Part One and the exposure work from Part Two.

As you read about each type of anxious thinking, examine your own thought processes to see which you do, and don't do. It can be quite hard at first to identify your thoughts – sometimes just a single word or image may flash though your mind so quickly that you are barely aware of it. You may not even see them as thoughts, instead you may identify them as feelings or physical sensations.

It can also be difficult to identify the external trigger that sets off the thoughts. Catching a glimpse of the cooker may set off thoughts about checking the gas, or walking towards a restaurant may set off the thoughts that lead to a panic attack, but the first thing you may normally be aware of is the adrenalin surge of Anxiety.

Working with thoughts

So keep a record for a week in your notebook – several times a day, examine your thoughts and write them down. If you have a bad Anxiety day, take extra trouble with this, but try to calm yourself before you pick up the notebook. Each time you make a note of your thoughts also mention the situation and the intensity of any feelings you had, both physical and emotional. Here's an example for someone with spider phobia:

Situation: leafing through magazine, saw photo of large spider.

Emotion: surge of fear, 6/10, feeling sweaty and shaky.

Thought: it's real, no it isn't it's a photo, but it might be, we could get spiders that big in this country and they might be poisonous.

When you've done this for a week, look back over your records and examine each thought. Ask yourself how much you believe it to be true, and how important that is.

Examination: thinking about it, I don't truly believe that we are going to get poisonous spiders in this country. I can see that it's not important enough to concern myself about.

Of course doing this once probably won't stop Anxiety in its tracks. In all of the following exercises that work with your thoughts, you will need to keep repeating them until you find your thoughts changing.

OCD and thoughts

If you have OCD you may feel that you already spend too much time with your thoughts, but if you work on your thoughts in the ways that we suggest, you will start to have a different relationship with them. Instead of believing the thoughts you will come to understand that they are generated by your Anxiety. All Anxiety is driven by the thoughts that go round and round in your head, but with OCD there is an extra element because the thoughts link in to beliefs, usually about preventing harm. There are various ways that this manifests itself, for instance:

- causing other people to become ill through not being clean enough

- causing an accident through not taking enough care

- causing harm through giving way to an impulse

- causing a problem through not checking documents, labels etc.

Any one of us can have thoughts like these from time to time. If you're cooking chicken for guests you might think about being careful to cook it right through to guard against food poisoning, or if you're getting irritated with a naughty child you might have a thought about giving them a good hard smack.

Research has shown that most of us are able to have these thoughts without getting upset or obsessed with them – we don't attach any importance to them. Someone with OCD is likely to attach enormous importance to thoughts of this type. The thought becomes mixed up with the dreaded consequence, something like 'if I don't cook this chicken right through then everyone will get food poisoning and it'll be my fault and they might need to go to hospital, they might even die and then I'd have killed someone' or 'I could easily smack this child if I'm not careful I will do it and if I don't watch myself I might really hurt them'.

If your thoughts run away with you like this it's only a small step to feeling as if you have really done the bad thing and are a bad person as a result. The next step happens when you tell yourself that you have to cancel out the bad thought, and stop it having a harmful effect – you might do this by having another type of thought, or by doing a ritualistic compulsion.

So, now that you know how to examine your own thoughts, let the trial commence.

GROUP MEMBERS TALK ABOUT NEGATIVE THOUGHTS

'I was stuck in a complicated mesh of anxieties. It was not unusual for me to think that I was losing my mind. The thoughts became embroidered emotionally with the most extraordinary possibilities and I would spend hours ruminating on what was to be.'
MARGARET

> *'I've had my breakfast, lunch, then tea.*
> *Preparing for them was agony.*
> *I can't believe that this is so real.*
> *To take so long over a simple meal.*
> *It has taken me the whole of the day.*
> *To keep those horrible thoughts at bay.'*

NORMAN

'Over several weeks I wrote down all my negative thoughts, and then made a tape where I repeated them and challenged each one.'
PEN

31 The First Two Charges Against Anxiety

Anxiety is charged with wilfully misinterpreting the world

People with Anxiety tend to make assumptions based on their intense feelings of panic and fear. In Part Two you saw how this can lead to anxious behaviours such as escape, avoidance or rituals. Behind those behaviours are anxious thoughts and a tendency to think the worst about bodily sensations, leading to the idea that not doing rituals will cause harm to befall another person or the idea that panic must be a heart attack.

There are three ways that Anxiety helps this process:

1. It causes you to overestimate the chances of danger.

2. It causes you to overestimate the size of the danger.

3. It causes you to underestimate your ability to cope with the danger.

Exercise

Write down in your notebook which of these your Anxiety is guilty of – it may be all of them, or just one. When you are doing your exposure work, you can mentally challenge your Anxiety by asking:

1. Is there really any risk of danger?

2. Is the danger really big enough to matter?

3. Surely I can cope with danger of this size?

Anxiety is charged with changing your thought patterns

Anxious thought patterns are a way of maintaining Anxiety, but they can be changed just as anxious behaviours can be changed. Let's look at three very common ones:

Scanning or hyper-vigilance

This means watching yourself all the time for alarming bodily sensations. You'll be on the look-out for danger and will be over-sensitive and detect it long before it really exists. If you have a phobia, you'll be on the alert for any hint of the feared object or situation. If you have OCD you'll constantly find new things that need cleaning or checking.

Fear of fear

Anxiety is so unpleasant and distressing that people will do anything to avoid it. If you've had a panic attack in a crowded bus, you will associate crowded buses with panic and start to dread getting on the bus if it looks full. If you were overwhelmed with fear when you tried to stop your rituals, then you'll be terrified of cutting them down in future. At this point you are afraid of feeling your fear just as much as the initial trigger for your problem – this is fear of fear.

Self-fulfilling prophesies

Anxiety tells you bad things are going to happen and lo and behold, they do. But was it inevitable? Let's look at the example of someone with social phobia. They enter a social situation feeling dreadfully self-conscious, and focusing on their own feelings. Perhaps they feel unable to make eye contact, and lurk unhappily on the edge of the proceedings. Their body language tells other people to leave them alone and they go home confirmed in their belief that nobody likes them.

Exercise

Write down in your notebook how your anxious thought processes affect you.

If you are **scanning**, then you are probably distracted and unable to focus on your daily life.

Fear of fear leads to avoidance and is the chief maintenance factor for panic, agoraphobia and social phobia.

Self-fulfilling prophesies will lead you to give up trying to recover, because you think the world doesn't hold anything worthwhile for you.

Scanning and fear of fear will both reduce as you persevere with your lifestyle changes and exposure work. With self-fulfilling prophecies you can set goals that include risking them coming true, because you'll also include the risk that they won't come true at all.

GROUP MEMBERS TALK ABOUT ANXIOUS THOUGHTS

'OCD is like superstition where you worry about the consequences of things in a way that's basically irrational.'
ANDREW

'In fact, instead of underestimating my ability to cope I sometimes overestimate it!'
JULIE

'I was constantly on the alert, watching my anxiety to see what trick it would pull next.'
MARGARET

> *'Now are my feet in the right position?*
> *To produce or prevent a dreaded situation.*
> *Don't get thinking of that again.*
> *It would be like going to the Lion's den.*
> *I must think of something else instead*
> *That should take away the fear and dread.'*

NORMAN

32 Anxiety is Charged with Distorting your Personality

There are many ways of describing the complicated entity that is each individual's personality. Introvert or Extrovert? Optimist or Pessimist? Inner directed or Other directed? One way that helps with understanding Anxiety is to think of your overall personality as being made up of a number of smaller personalities, rather like a large box of assorted sweets. Perhaps when you are at work you are organised and efficient, while at home you are relaxed and caring. Or you may be very sociable with the people you meet at your local sports club, but quite withdrawn if you find yourself in a fancy restaurant.

These smaller personalities are called sub-personalities and they are all equally important to making up the unique being that is you, and in a healthy person they all have their uses and balance each other out. However, if you have Anxiety it's likely that one or more of the four sub-personalities described below has got out of hand and has become far too dominant.

The worrier

Worrying is part of the human ability to look into the future and make decisions based on the likelihood of something happening – worrying that it looks like rain will cause you to take an umbrella for instance. Also you can look into the past – worrying that you made a bad job of something will cause you to try harder the next time.

However, if your Worrier becomes too dominant you're likely to start assuming that something will always go wrong. You'll always be on the lookout for trouble. A Worrier's typical thoughts start 'What if...' 'What if I pass out?' 'What if there are germs on my hands?' 'What if my helper abandons me?'

The critic

Being able to criticise yourself is a useful skill and helps you improve your performance. How smug and self-satisfied we'd all be if we didn't have a critic inside us.

But a Critic who has started to run wild will lead to you being preoccupied with what other people think about you. You'll always judge yourself in the worst way and never give yourself the benefit of the doubt. A Critic's typical thoughts are 'I'm so stupid,' or 'I'm such a failure.'

The victim

Victim is a fairly negative word and yet we all have bad times that we know weren't our fault. Recognising when we've been victimised helps us to deal with the bad experience, and reminds us to nurture ourselves when it's over.

This is fine but it's not helpful if your dominant mindset is that of the Victim. You'll feel helpless and hopeless, and unable to take responsibility for yourself or to control your life. A Victim's thought patterns are along the lines of 'I can't manage it' 'What's the point of trying?' 'What's the use?'.

The perfectionist

The desire to improve is one of the bedrocks of human progress, and there are times when a perfectionist streak will lead us to achievements that we never thought were possible.

But, rather like the Critic, a dominant Perfectionist will tell you that you'll never be good enough. Your sense of self-worth will depend on your achievements, your status, or simply on being liked, and yet you'll never feel that you've got enough of any of these. Perfectionist thoughts tend to include commands such as 'I must do better', 'I should have done X' 'I ought to do Y'.

Exercise

Read through the four personality types and decide which ones your Anxiety has enlisted to help. Make a list of all the thoughts that your anxious sub-personalities throw at you. Decide which one is the most important and use the examples below to start the process of putting it back in its place.

Ways of countering the four personalities

The way to deal with the negative thoughts that your anxious sub-personalities are constantly throwing at you is to find a way to put the ball back in their court. This is called countering. Work your way through your list of thoughts and devise an answer to each one. Here are some examples of thoughts and counters:

Worrier

What if I make a fool of myself? *So what? I can cope with being a fool if it helps me get better.*

What if I have a heart attack? *All my tests are negative and I really need to do my exposure work.*

Critic

I'm a useless parent. *I'm the best parent I can be.*

Other people don't get in this mess. *They must do – they wouldn't run helplines just for me.*

I've never been good at anything. *I'm good at being me and that's all I need.*

Victim

It's all my parents' fault. *I'm an adult, I'll take responsibility now.*

What's the point of trying, I'll never get better. *If I don't try, I'll never know.*

I'll never find someone to love me. *I'll start with loving myself.*

Perfectionist

I ought to have got over this by now. *Who says? It takes as long as it takes.*

I shouldn't need to ask for help with the kids. *Superwoman is a myth. I'm human.*

I must deal with this on my own. *It's OK to ask for help.*

As you can see, the counters are all positive statements. Your brain will take them on board much more easily if they are expressed that way, so don't use negatives For example, when countering 'I'm a useless parent' don't say 'I'm not a useless parent' – the words 'useless parent' are still there nagging at you so take them right out and say boldly 'I'm the best parent I can be.'

For combating 'should' statements, try being more polite to yourself – as if you were talking to another person. Instead of 'I should...' try saying 'it would be nice if...'. Don't get bogged down when you use counters – counter each thought once, and then move on.

GROUP MEMBERS TALK ABOUT SUB-PERSONALITIES

'I'm mainly a critic, although I can be a bit of a worrier and a perfectionist. I've never tried to consciously change this about myself.'
ANDREA

'I'm not a critic, victim or perfectionist but I am a worrier.'
ANDREW

'I'd say I was a worrier, mainly about my work, and I can be a bit of a critic.'
BRIDGET

'I'm a worrier and a perfectionist, but the perfectionist is dominant.'
JULIE

'My dominant sub-personality is the worrier – oh those perishing "What-ifs".'
PEN

'I'm not a worrier, I'm mostly laid back. I am a critic, I laugh at myself. I used to be a victim but now I refuse to call myself a victim. I'm now a survivor and a bit of a perfectionist.'
SARAH

'I'm a Victim, because my dad abused me most of my life. I was adopted and he always said nobody would believe me if I told because I was adopted.'
WENDY

33 Anxiety is Charged with Extreme Thinking

Each sub-personality has its own brand of twisted thinking (or cognitive distortion). There are other thought habits that Anxiety creates, so the trial continues.

If you think back to the time before you had Anxiety, you'll see that your thinking has changed considerably. Even if you were always a worrier, you didn't worry as much as you do now, and your thoughts didn't escalate like they do now. Extreme thinking is one of Anxiety's favourite tricks, and it comes in four forms.

Overestimating a bad outcome

When you look into the future, you assume that there will always be a negative result to anything you do. Maybe you feel like that about exposure work, and you expect to fail at every goal. Even when you succeed, you think it was a fluke, or a one-off. Typical thoughts are:
'I'll panic and make a fool of myself.'
'I'll be the only one in the class to fail the exam.'
'If I don't get this job I won't get another chance.'

Catastrophising

As you would expect, this means seeing a catastrophe around every corner. The bad outcome from category 1 is, in your mind, always going to be the absolute worst outcome possible – even if you're not sure what. Typical catastrophic thoughts are:
'If I panic it'll be the end of everything.'
'If anything goes wrong I'll never live it down.'
'They'll never speak to me again.'

Unrealistic expectations

Even though Anxiety is keeping you chained to your restricted life, you may still have unrealistic expectations of yourself. For instance someone who is housebound, and who contemplates their first trip outside, will set themselves an impossibly difficult challenge, often on the basis that anything less is hardly worth bothering with. Typical unrealistic thoughts are:

'I should be able to do this.'

'I can't be bothered with little steps.'

All-or-nothing thinking

This means seeing the world in black and white terms – things are either right or wrong, good or bad, with no shades of grey in between. Typical all-or-nothing thoughts are:

'I must be 100% right or I'm a failure.'

'I got one thing wrong and that ruined everything.'

Ways of countering extreme thinking

As you can see there is quite a lot of overlap between these four categories, and it's likely that you'll identify yourself as doing more than one type of extreme thinking. Make a list of your own particular extreme thoughts, and then work out ways of countering them. Here are some examples:

Overestimating a bad outcome

'I'll be the only one in the class to fail the exam.' *So what? The important thing is to sit the exam and do the best I can.*

Catastrophising

'If anything goes wrong I'll never live it down.' *Yes I will. It's only embarrassment, and I can cope with that.*

Unrealistic expectations

'I should be able to do this.' *I need to try, that's all.*

All-or-nothing thinking

'I got one thing wrong and that ruined everything.' *Everything else was OK, so I did pretty well.*

You may recognise this mindset if you have ever been a parent, or worked with children. Anxiety does, in some ways, take us back to childhood, where the world is big and scary and there are bogeymen in dark places. Don't dismiss this, or feel ashamed of it – but do use countering statements to help the frightened child in you let go of its extreme thinking.

GROUP MEMBERS TALK ABOUT EXTREME THINKING

'Do I overestimate the chances of something bad happening? Oh God yes. This is the crux of my OCD. These days I'm much better at risk assessment and estimating the likelihood of it happening. And I do catastrophise, but I don't think I have the other negative thought patterns. Do I use "should" statements? I'm not aware of doing this but I may be subconsciously doing it.'
ANDREW

'On the whole I don't have a negative mindset but I do sometimes overestimate the chances of something bad happening. I do use "should" and "ought" statements to myself.'
BRIDGET

'I do overestimate the chances of something bad happening and I do catastrophise – they are both demons for me.'
PEN

'I do overestimate the chances of something bad happening quite a lot. I catastrophise, underestimate my ability to cope, filter out the positive.'
SARAH

'I used to catastrophise, but I don't now. I have tried to change my mindset. Now I've lost both my parents and my brother and I think "I am free and I can do what I want."'
WENDY

34 Anxiety is Charged with Selective Attention

The world is a complicated place, and we lead complicated lives, and there is always a tendency for our world view to change, almost minute by minute. If you get home from work tired, with no food in the fridge, you're likely to feel fairly miserable and negative about the evening ahead – when the phone rings and it's a friend on their way round with a pizza to share you're likely to change your mind in an instant. In both cases your attention is selective – either focusing on the negative, or the positive. Someone with Anxiety is likely to be stuck with one or more of the following types of negative selective attention.

Over-generalising

This means that you assume that one bad experience will always lead to others – this is how a phobia develops, when after one bad time in a certain situation you assume that the same thing will always happen every time in the future. Over-generalising usually includes words like 'never', 'always' and 'every', so typical examples are:
'I'll never manage this goal.'
'I'm always the one who struggles.'

Filtering

Filtering means selecting one aspect of an experience and focusing on that – and of course for an Anxiety sufferer this is going to mean filtering out the positive and focusing on the negative. This can be very like all-or-nothing thinking, where you focus entirely on one bad thing and ignore all the good things. Typical filtering thoughts are:
'I made a mess of that driving lesson, I'll never pass my test.'
'I had a bad day yesterday, I'll never get better.'

Discounting the positive

This is a companion to filtering, and the dominant word in this thought process is 'but'. It doesn't matter how many good things have come your way, there will always be a 'but' as you knock back the good and focus on the bad. Typical thoughts are:

'I cut down my checking yesterday morning, but I was as bad as ever in the afternoon.'

'Lots of people recover from Anxiety, but I'll be the exception.'

Magnifying and minimising

This kind of selective attention makes bad things big and good things small, so it's really a combination of filtering and discounting the positive. Typical thoughts are:

'I had the most horrendous panic attack on Tuesday, and even though Wednesday and Thursday were okay I can't forget it.'

'I'm the worst case of anxiety ever, and the progress I've made so far just doesn't count.'

Ways of countering selective attention

Selective attention on the negative means that you downplay your successes and play up your failures. You ignore the evidence, or choose to misinterpret it – but Anxiety is on trial here, and you need to be objective about the evidence.

Finding counters for these kinds of thoughts is a question of persuading yourself to accept the evidence at face value, for example:

Over-generalising

I'm always the one who struggles. *If I look around me I'll see that other people have difficulties too.*

Filtering

I had a bad day yesterday, I'll never get better. *I will look through my notebook and see how many good days I had, because they are just as important.*

Discounting the positive

I cut down my checking yesterday morning, but I was as bad as ever in the afternoon. *It felt great yesterday morning, and it proves that I can do it.*

Magnifying and minimising

I'm the worst case of Anxiety ever, and the progress I've made so far just doesn't count. *Even the smallest progress counts, even the fact of having a go at recovery counts, and even the worst case of Anxiety ever can get better.*

GROUP MEMBERS TALK ABOUT SELECTIVE ATTENTION

'I do have negative thought patterns but I'm working on it. I use positive self-talk and affirmations.'
ANDREA

'I used to do most of the negative thought habits, such as catastrophising, generalising from one bad experience or using "should" statements, but now I try to stop myself.'
JULIE

'I do generalise from one bad experience but I think it's very subliminal.'
PEN

'I do generalise from one bad experience. I failed the driving test first time. The examiner was tough on me, and undermined my confidence.'
SARAH

---

35 The Final Charges Against Anxiety

Anxiety is charged with distorting your intuition

Nobody is quite sure how intuition works, and intuitive thoughts seem to come from nowhere and to be very powerful. Your brain has been busy at such a deep level that you aren't consciously aware of the thought processes, but nevertheless there are thought processes, and Anxiety can bring its influence to bear on them just the same as any others.

There are two main types of distorted intuition:

Emotional reasoning

This means using your feelings to make a judgement or decision. Sometimes it's entirely appropriate to do this, for instance in the area of personal relationships. However many people with Anxiety use emotional reasoning inappropriately, and rely on their feelings to guide them. Typical thoughts are:

'I won't do my exposure today because I don't feel like it.'

'I feel useless, so that means I am useless.'

Jumping to conclusions

This means making decisions about other people – what they meant when they said a certain thing, why they did a certain thing, what they were thinking when they glanced across at you and so on. Anxiety makes sure that you always assume the worst, and yet you are just as likely to be wrong as right. Typical thoughts are:

'She ignored me, she must hate me.'

'He's staring at me, I must be doing something odd.'

If someone you know passes you without speaking, your intuition, coloured by Anxiety, might well lead you to assume they were angry with you for some reason. And yet they might well have simply not seen you, or been sunk into their own thoughts and worries. And you cannot possibly know what a stranger is thinking when they glance at you – it could be 'what a weirdo'(in which case it's their problem, not yours) but equally it could be 'I wonder where they got their jacket?'

Anxiety is charged with creating self-reproach

This is the last item on the charge sheet. Anxiety says that everything is your fault, and makes sure you feel badly about it too.

Taking it personally

A middle-aged woman took her elderly father to the dentist. The receptionist said to him 'isn't it kind of your sister to give you a lift?' The woman was mortified, and cried bitter tears when she got home. But why didn't it occur to her that maybe it was that her father looked young, not that she looked old? In fact what she didn't know was that the receptionist had broken her glasses, and was struggling through the day without them. This is 'taking it personally' – like 'jumping to conclusions', you are just as likely to be wrong as right.

Blaming yourself

Do you feel responsible for everything that happens to your nearest and dearest? Do you try to cover every eventuality, and make sure they are okay at all times? And do you blame yourself when things go wrong, or they aren't happy? And do you think that having Anxiety is all your own fault?

Name-calling

We all beat ourselves up from time to time, using words like 'fool', 'idiot' and maybe a few unprintable ones too, but Anxiety can persuade you to be far too hard on yourself, so that you constantly think things like 'I'm so clumsy, so lazy, so forgetful' and so on. Clearly this links in with perfectionism, and criticism.

Wishful thinking

This means you constantly compare yourself with other people and think that if only you were more like them you'd be able to throw off your Anxiety. Whether you wish to be better looking, cleverer, younger, fitter or thinner it all comes down to dissatisfaction with yourself.

Ways of countering distorted intuition and self-reproach

Distorted intuition and self-reproach are all about how you see yourself in relation to the world, and other people. Your own reactions are of overwhelming importance to you but by focusing on them so much you can lose sight of other ways of viewing a situation. Here are some ways of countering this tendency:

Emotional reasoning

Ask yourself 'Are my feelings appropriate here? Are they relevant?'

Jumping to conclusions

Consider if there could be another explanation for the situation. Accept that you might be wrong about other people's reasons for behaving as they do.

Taking it personally

Again, look at the situation and see if there could be another explanation, one that doesn't involve you.

Blaming yourself

Feeling responsible is one of the hardest things to let go of, and for some people it goes to the very core of their being. It might help to look at it from the other person's point of view – maybe they don't want you to make everything okay for them. Maybe they'd be happier if they could take responsibility for their own life.

Name calling

Make a list of your favourite name calling words and resolve to take them out of your vocabulary. Tell yourself you're banned from ever using them again.

Wishful thinking

By whose standards are you judging yourself? Learn to love and respect yourself. Contradict your 'if only...' thoughts with 'I'm fine the way I am'.

GROUP MEMBERS TALK ABOUT NEGATIVE THOUGHT PATTERNS

'...those of you who put yourselves down as worthless and a burden, don't believe in such rubbish.'
MARGARET

'I use emotional reasoning and "should" statements.'
SARAH

'I did used to generalise from one bad experience, filter out the positive, use emotional reasoning and 'should' statements – but not now! I didn't work to stop myself, it just happened naturally. To be on your own suddenly at 60, that makes you do things like go to the shops.'
WENDY

---

36 Another Approach – Logical Argument

The trial is over, and while the jury's considering the verdict we're going to look at another way of working with your thought processes.

Socrates was born nearly 2,500 years ago, and he created a way of questioning that is still useful today. He used to encourage his students to question everything in a strict and rigorous way that was designed to make them think for themselves instead of just going along with their first ideas on the subject, or believing what they were told. This approach doesn't come naturally to most of us but it is a useful way to put anxious thinking under the spotlight. Think of it as a truth test.

These are the kinds of questions to ask:

What are the facts?
What is the evidence for this thought being true?
Has this been true in the past?
What are the chances of this happening, or of this being true?
What is the worst thing that could happen?
Why is that the worst thing, and why is it so bad?
What would I do if the worst happened?
Am I looking at the whole picture?
Am I being objective?

An example of Socratic questioning

Here is an example of Socratic questioning for someone who fears having a panic attack at a parent-teacher evening.

What are the facts? *I have to see the teacher for ten minutes on Tuesday but I can't go because I'll have a panic attack.*

What is the evidence for this thought being true? *I had a panic attack at the doctor's last week, and also when I was waiting at the school gate the other day.*

Has this been true in the past? *I nearly had a panic attack at the last parent-teacher evening but I made an excuse and left in time. Before that I was fine but I didn't have Anxiety then.*

What are the chances of this happening, or of this being true? *I think the chances of me having a panic attack are very high.*

What is the worst thing that could happen? *If I have a panic attack and the teacher sees me they'll think I'm a bad parent and a stupid person.*

Why is that the worst thing, and why is it so bad? *I don't know why it's the worst thing, it just is.*

What would I do if the worst happened? *I'd run out of the school and I'd feel stupid and humiliated.*

Am I looking at the whole picture? *I can't, I'm only looking at me and the fear of panic.*

Am I being objective? *No, probably not.*

You can see that as the questions proceed the flaws in the argument emerge. Is it really the worst thing that can happen if a teacher sees someone being upset? Clearly it isn't, there are much worse things that can happen to someone, and so the answer to the next question is 'I don't know why it's the worst thing' followed by the admission that they aren't looking at the whole picture, or being objective.

Once you have admitted this, you can reassess the answers. 'I'll have a panic attack' changes to 'I might have a panic attack.' 'The chances are high' changes to 'the chances are less than 100%'. 'I'd feel humiliated' changes to 'I'd find a way to cope' and so on.

More questions to ask yourself

Socratic questioning can be applied to all types of anxious thinking. In addition, you can ask yourself other questions that will help you be more objective such as:

Are there other ways of looking at this?

If someone I knew had this thought, what would I say to them?

What are the alternative ways of approaching this?

The parent with the fear of panic might answer as follows:

Are there other ways of looking at this? *I suppose I could tell myself it's only ten minutes, and to give it a try. I could tell the teacher about my Anxiety problem, maybe they'd understand.*

If someone I knew had this thought, what would I say to them? *I'd tell them not to be so hard on themselves. I'd tell them we all have problems from time to time and I'd tell them not to worry about the teacher's reaction, teachers are tough types who aren't easily thrown.*

What are the alternative ways of approaching this? *I could see it as one of my goals.*

Socratic argument and OCD

Using the Socratic questioning technique can be very helpful in breaking out of OCD's illogical thoughts. Here is an example for someone with a fear of losing control and harming another person.

What are the facts? *I can't drive my car because I'm sure that if I do I will cause an accident, and I'll have to go back and check my route.*

What is the evidence for this thought being true? *I failed my test twice, and I have scratched my car on a gatepost.*

Has this been true in the past? *Somebody drove into the back of my car once. They said it was my fault.*

What are the chances of this happening, or of this being true? *I don't know, people have car accidents all the time.*

What is the worst thing that could happen? *I could cause an accident where somebody dies.*

Why is that the worst thing, and why is it so bad? *It's the worst thing because it would be my fault, and I couldn't live with myself.*

What would I do if the worst happened? *I'd go mad, or something.*

Am I looking at the whole picture? *No. I know that most people actually don't have accidents, but I don't know how they stop themselves worrying about it.*

Am I being objective? *I suppose not. I drove for nine years before OCD made me give up.*

What alternative explanation might there be for me having this thought? *That I become anxious when I get in the car, and then have these thoughts.*

What would be the worst that could happen? *I will feel very anxious but that's all.*

Once again the thoughts don't stand up to careful questioning. There is no real evidence that this person is an unsafe driver and there is no objective reason for them to give up driving. Equally they won't be miraculously cured of OCD just because of the Socratic questioning, but once they have accepted that there could be an alternative explanation – i.e. the thoughts are produced by their Anxiety – then the method described below can be used to test this out with the aim of easing them gradually back behind the wheel.

37 The Verdict

The jury returns, the verdict is in, and Anxiety is guilty, no doubt about it. The details of the verdict will be different for each person, since Anxiety doesn't treat us all the same. It can be a bully, a demon, an authority figure, a false friend. Only you can decide what your Anxiety is guilty of.

You've spent some time in court now, studying Anxiety, and hearing how it speaks to you. Did you recognise anything about it? Very often when people are asked to listen to their anxious thoughts, they realise that the voice doesn't belong to them at all – it's the voice of an adult from their childhood, one who nagged, or bullied, or put them down all the time. Maybe it's the voice of someone who truly cared, such as a parent or grandparent, but who had a negative way of showing it.

If you can identify your Anxiety in this way, you can use that knowledge as part of your recovery. You can tell the nag or the bully to be quiet, in fact you can tell them to get out of your head entirely. If it's the voice of someone who loved you, you can still explain that you don't need their negative remarks any more.

If you don't recognise the voice in this way, you can still characterise your Anxiety in whatever way feels right to you – call it something, such as Bully, or Bossyboots, so that you can talk to it and tell it to pipe down.

Changing your anxious thinking

It's time to set up the next part of the recovery programme, which aims to change your anxious thinking. Look back through your notebook and

pick out the types of anxious thinking that you are prone to. Here is a
reminder checklist:

- ☐ overestimating the chances of danger
- ☐ overestimating the size of the danger
- ☐ underestimating your ability to cope with the danger
- ☐ scanning
- ☐ fear of fear
- ☐ self-fulfilling prophecies
- ☐ worrier
- ☐ critic
- ☐ victim
- ☐ perfectionist
- ☐ overestimating a bad outcome
- ☐ catastrophising
- ☐ unrealistic expectations
- ☐ all-or-nothing thinking
- ☐ over-generalising
- ☐ filtering
- ☐ discounting the positive
- ☐ magnifying/minimising
- ☐ emotional reasoning
- ☐ jumping to conclusions
- ☐ taking it personally
- ☐ blaming yourself
- ☐ name calling
- ☐ wishful thinking.

Checklist – coping skills for cognitive work

In exposure work the coping skills are all about helping you manage your
Anxiety so that you get through your goals. When you are trying to
change your thought processes you need coping skills that will give you
the confidence to let go of anxious thinking. Here are some tips:

☐ Make a list of your strengths and positive qualities. Don't include anything negative.

☐ Tell yourself that what you perceive as your weaknesses and defects are all part of being human. Nobody is perfect.

☐ Remember that you and your behaviour are not the same thing. Even if you do make a mistake, that doesn't make you a bad person.

☐ Understand your Anxiety. Knowledge is power, and now that you understand the physical signals of Anxiety, where they come from and why, you don't need to be so alarmed about them.

☐ Have compassion for yourself. Instead of blaming yourself, tell yourself that there are probably good reasons why you have anxious thoughts.

GROUP MEMBERS TALK ABOUT COPING SKILLS

'I have a list that I read every day. I don't let the negative stop me doing things.'
ANDREA

'I try to change negative thoughts to positive ones and I use affirmations. I'm a fan of Emile Coué with his "Every day, in every way, I am getting better and better" and one of my favourites is, "Whatever life throws at me today I will handle beautifully".'
ANDREW

'When I feel myself becoming negative I use positive self-talk, and the little catch phrase I use to myself is "I don't need that".'
JULIE

'I devised an imaginary cupboard where I would put my worries and close the door on them. It worked beautifully provided my attention to what I was doing was absorbing.'
MARGARET

'I do try to change my mind set by challenging my constant self-talk.'
PEN

'To stop myself overestimating the chances of something bad happening I think positive. For catastrophising I now go for it anyway and tell myself what happens will happen. It usually isn't so bad, so I'm learning not to always expect the worst. With underestimating my ability to cope, I don't let it stop me trying. I'm learning to accept positive feedback from other people and working on emotional reasoning.'
SARAH

'I realise how important it is to have a goal to aim for.'
TERESA

'I tell that bully Anxiety I'm going out and I'm not taking it with me.'
WENDY

38 Other Techniques to Use to Change Your Thinking

We've already shown you how to create counter statements to your negative thoughts, and how to use Socratic arguments. There are a few other techniques that you can use, and you should choose the ones that appeal to you most:

Challenge your thoughts

Say to yourself 'I don't have to accept that thought.'

Use affirmations

These are statements that you repeat to yourself regularly. The great original affirmation is 'every day in every way I am growing better and better.' It can feel pretty silly to look in the mirror and repeat this sort of thing, but all we can say is, it does work, so do it.

Get a better perspective

Instead of thinking in black and white terms (failure or success, stupid or competent, great or awful) learn to value the shades of grey in-between. For instance, to change all-or-nothing thinking, write down the two extremes and draw a line between them. Decide where you are on the line and tell yourself that where you are is okay.

Do a cost-benefit analysis

This simply means looking at the advantages and disadvantages of something. Ask yourself 'How does this negative thought help me? How does it hurt me?' If the hurt is greater than the help, then you can let the thought go. Remember, it's only a thought.

Relax

Use your breathing and relaxation techniques to calm yourself when thoughts start to spiral.

When you are talking to yourself in new ways, or creating counters, challenges and affirmations, remember the following guidelines:

- Use the first person – use the word 'I'.
- Use the present tense – say 'I can do this' not 'I will do this'.
- Use positive statements – say 'I can do this', not 'I won't be beaten'.
- Find something you do believe in, don't just use empty words.
- Don't engage in arguments with yourself.

Testing your cognitive work

Now you're going to put your new knowledge to the test in a live situation. We suggest you choose a goal from your exposure list that you have already begun to master and repeat it purely to test out your new thinking. If you have OCD, then read the example below.

Look down the checklist in Chapter 37 and choose three types of negative thinking that you are ready to work on. For each one, write a brief statement that will give you support. Here are some examples:

Underestimating your ability to cope: *I can cope even if I start to feel panicky.*

Perfectionism: *It's okay to make mistakes, I can learn from them.*

Blaming yourself: *I can let go of feeling responsible.*

It might help to write these down on a small card to carry with you, to remind yourself.

Now repeat your goal – because you have done it before your physical Anxiety will be lower, and you will be able to pay attention to your thoughts. Follow this procedure:

- start the goal
- catch yourself in the act of negative thinking
- pause for a moment and ask whether you want to do this to yourself
- relax
- use one of the techniques listed above
- mentally repeat your supporting statement
- continue with the goal.

With practice you will become quicker at spotting the negative thoughts and interrupting them.

Cognitive work and OCD

Ask yourself the question: *Do my rituals really make a difference or are they driven by my Anxiety?*

Facing this possibility can feel very uncomfortable, after all you give over a large chunk of your life to OCD rituals, do you really want to find out that it was all pointless? Of course it wasn't pointless, but you may have been missing the point – focusing on your obsessive thoughts instead of dealing with your Anxiety. If you can reach an understanding that the rituals do not, in fact, make a difference, then you can free up some energy for working on your Anxiety.

Let's look at the situation objectively.

There are two ways of looking at your thoughts. On the one hand there may be a real danger that you are able to prevent by doing your rituals. On the other hand you may have the thoughts because you're anxious, and the rituals don't make any difference to what happens in the real world.

The next step is to test the theories in a live situation. Start by keeping a record of one day during which you do your rituals. Make a list of all the people that you feel you are protecting with the rituals, and make a list of any bad things that happen to them on that day. This record will provide you with a basis for comparison.

Testing cognitive work for OCD

Next, choose a risk that you feel is real, but manageable. For example, someone with a cleaning ritual might choose to stop cleaning the living room while still cleaning the kitchen and bathroom on the basis that the greatest risk of infection lies in those two rooms. Write down in your notebook exactly what you intend to do, and what you expect the outcome to be for each of the two theories:

Example:

Test: *I won't do my cleaning ritual in the living room for one day.*

Theory A prediction: *Someone in the family will be ill, or have an accident (this would include a list of the people concerned, and a list of specific bad things that might happen).*

Theory B prediction: *I will be anxious as I imagine all the danger.*

While you are conducting a test like this you can expect to feel anxious, so you need to have coping techniques ready. Keep a record of your Anxiety throughout the test, so that you can trace how it peaks and then starts to die away. Also keep a record of any bad things that happen to the people on the list – there will always be some negative events in any family, so it's important that you only include those things that were in your original prediction.

Compare the two sets of records. Were there really more of the specified bad things on the day of the test? Or was it just your Anxiety that was bad?

After the session – all anxiety disorders

When you've finished the session, write it up in your notebook in the usual way. Give your Anxiety a score out of 10, and note whether monitoring your thoughts made any difference.

This will probably seem quite tedious at first, but after a while it will become second nature to monitor your negative thoughts and put a stop to them as soon as they start. If you persist, eventually they won't even start.

Brooding

Some people with Anxiety develop a tendency to worry at their thoughts. This is especially common in OCD, but people with panic, GAD and phobias can also find that they spend long periods of time locked into their thoughts, probably being very inactive, and not really connecting with their daily life.

If you recognise yourself in this, you'll need to take particular care with your cognitive work. There is no need to spend hours monitoring your thoughts, arguing with yourself or haggling with yourself over just how much work you're able to do.

When you are doing cognitive exercises, keep your mental responses short and to the point. The value comes from repeating them, just like with exposure work, but unlike exposure work it is better to keep your sessions short. At first your Anxiety may well send nagging thoughts (just like a child in a car repeating 'are we nearly there yet?' endlessly) but all you need to do is give your chosen response and keep on with your planned session.

GROUP MEMBERS TALK ABOUT MAKING CHANGES

'... seeing things from a different angle, trying not to be hard on myself, giving myself some leeway.'
ANDREW

'I have tried to change my mindset. I tell myself I can only do so much. I also tell myself how much time I can spend on something, and that helps me to stop and walk away from it.'
JULIE

'It's easy for any of us to develop the habit of using the expression "what if?" This is where we need to change our habits and replace this expression with the words "so what!" Consider the following question. "What if I make a mistake?" Now compare this with a similar question, "So what if I make a mistake?"'
NORMAN

'I'll take the driving test again and be better prepared!'
SARAH

'I take any opportunity I can to help with self-awareness.'
TERESA

'I don't underestimate my ability to cope, because I've coped twice with difficult bereavements. We're all a lot stronger than we think we are.'
WENDY

39 More about Thought Processes

Imagine you're sitting on the grass on a lovely summer's day. Without really thinking about it, you pick a dandelion flower and examine it. It's not especially pretty, and it's spoiling the look of the lawn, so you pull the leaves from the plant as well. Now the lawn looks better, but any gardener will tell you that a dandelion will recover even if you pull its leaves off, so you grab a trowel and dig down into the soil to get the root out. It's long and tough but at last you get it out, and now you know that dandelion won't be growing back in your lawn.

You can compare your anxious thought processes to the dandelion plant.

At the top are the automatic thoughts that pop into your head when you're feeling anxious. 'What if I pass out?' 'Supposing something bad happens and it's my fault?' 'I have to get out of here!' These thoughts are like the flower.

Next are the cognitive distortions that we've already looked at, everything from all-or-nothing thinking to wishful thinking. They are like the leaves of the plant.

All of these thought processes are fed by something deeper, the roots of the plant. They are known as core beliefs and they can be very difficult to dig up, just like a dandelion root, but the unhelpful ones are feeding your Anxiety and probably making it difficult for you to complete your recovery.

Core beliefs

Core beliefs are formed in the earliest part of your life and they relate to three things:

- judgements about yourself
- judgements about other people
- judgements about the world.

So examples of core beliefs might be:

- I'm fine as I am
- other people generally mean well
- the world's my oyster.

Unfortunately someone with Anxiety is most likely to have negative core beliefs, for instance:

- I'm not lovable
- other people always let you down
- life isn't fair.

Very often these beliefs are so deeply ingrained that we're not aware of them, or if we are, they feel like universal truths. Core beliefs are formed very early in life. They can come from the people around you, or the culture you grow up in, or your life experiences. So if you are brought up by your parents to believe that 'boys don't cry' or if in your culture 'girls are second class citizens' then you'll find it hard to resist that conditioning. It's the same with life experiences: if a parent dies or leaves you when you are young you may develop your own core belief that 'people always abandon me'.

Identifying your core beliefs

One way of identifying core beliefs is to look at your cognitive distortions and see what might be underlying and feeding them.

COGNITIVE DISTORTION	CORE BELIEF
Overestimating the chances of danger	Bad things always happen
Overestimating the size of the danger	Bad things are always worse than you expect
Underestimating your ability to cope with the danger	I'm useless
Scanning	You have to watch out for trouble
Fear of fear	The world is scary
Self-fulfilling prophecies	I'm sure to make a fool of myself
Worrier	If it can go wrong, it will
Critic	I'm incompetent
Victim	Life isn't fair
Perfectionist	I'm useless and need to try harder
Overestimating a bad outcome	I never get a break
Catastrophising	If it can get worse, it will
Unrealistic expectations	It's all my fault
All-or-nothing thinking	Only 100% will do
Over-generalising	My life is a mess
Filtering	The world is a bad place
Discounting the positive	Anyone could have done that – I'm not really any good
Magnifying/minimising	Everyone is smarter than I am My contribution is pathetic
Emotional reasoning	Because I feel scared, it must be dangerous
Jumping to conclusions	If someone disagrees with me, they think I'm stupid
Taking it personally	It's my fault that things happen
Blaming yourself	I'm to blame
Name calling	I'm a loser
Wishful thinking	I'm unlovable

GROUP MEMBERS TALK

*'I can see that my mother was very anxious and terrified of illness
and I did develop a health anxiety.'*
ANDREA

*'I have this approach that I don't think other people will be interested
in my feelings so I keep quiet. I also tend not to trust people with my
feelings.'*
ANDREW

40 The Vicious Circle

Now you can see how anxious thinking is a vicious circle, with your core beliefs as the source of the energy that drives the circle round and round. Remember there are three elements to the thoughts – your surface (or automatic) thoughts, your underlying assumptions, and your core beliefs.

For instance, here's how the circle might work for someone whose core belief is 'I'm useless':

- They feel their heart thumping, and their breathing get faster.

- Automatically they think 'it's panic – what if I can't handle it?'

- Their underlying assumption causes them to think 'I should be able to handle it.'

- Their core belief causes them to think 'I'm useless, I can't handle it, I need to get out.'

- They then leave the situation because they believe they can't handle the panic.

- This reinforces their belief that they are useless, and the circle is ready for another spin the next time.

Core beliefs that drive the vicious circle

The internal logic that drives the vicious circle clearly isn't objective, but it can be very difficult to tease out the twists and turns of the belief. There is no difficulty in understanding the effects of negative core beliefs

– they undermine your self-esteem and sense of self-worth. If you are always measuring yourself against your core beliefs and finding yourself lacking, then you will never rate yourself very highly.

These kinds of beliefs are self-fulfilling – if you believe that you can't cope, then the chances are that you won't cope. Counsellors have a saying 'if you do what you've always done, then you'll get what you've always got.' In other words, if you keep telling yourself negative things, then you'll keep failing in the very ways that you don't want to fail.

Negative core beliefs are often related to achievement, acceptability, trust or control.

- **Achievement**: 'I have to do everything perfectly or else I'm a failure.'

- **Acceptability**: 'everyone has to be pleased with me or else I'm not good enough.'

- **Trust**: 'if I trust, I will be hurt.'

- **Control**: 'if I ask for help I'm weak' or 'if I feel anxious I'm losing control.'

OCD and core beliefs

People with OCD often have core beliefs around perfection, responsibility and punishment that are linked together. A core belief around perfection might be 'I must be perfect' which turns into 'I must be perfect or I'll be punished' or 'it's my responsibility to make myself perfect.' Responsibility produces 'I have to stop bad things happening' and 'if I don't stop bad things happening I deserve to be punished'.

OCD rituals are sometimes a way of stopping bad things from happening, and sometimes they are the way the person punishes themselves for failing to be perfect or failing to stop the bad things happening.

In the quest to be perfect someone with OCD can blame themselves for any thoughts they have which they judge to be 'bad' thoughts and may feel they should be punished for having those thoughts. Research suggests that most people have thoughts concerning harm or other bad things but that they pay very little attention to them. Someone with OCD may also come to believe that just by having the thoughts they can cause bad things to happen.

Although the thoughts and rituals may seem quite strange, psychologists believe that they developed for good reasons – usually as ways for a child to get through a difficult situation. They are not appropriate for an adult, but they persist even so, or emerge at times of stress – see Chapter 41 for an explanation of this.

GROUP MEMBERS TALK

'My feeling is, if this is what I've had, now I know how to deal with it – it's simply a reaction to some stress, it's not a physical illness. It's not that scary to me now because I believe the doctors.'
BRIDGET

'I have often wondered if, because I am sensitised to anxiety, things somehow become harder than they need to be as some kind of test.'
JULIE

'We are not living in hell from choice but have an anxiety illness. Who would want to live like this?'
MARGARET

'I know that when I was in the wrong mindset, I used to be determined that the treatments wouldn't help.'
SARAH

41 Working on Your Negative Core Beliefs

Challenging your core beliefs can make you feel very uncomfortable, so be kind to yourself while you are doing this work. If you already feel ashamed, guilty or inadequate because of your core beliefs, then telling yourself that your world view is all wrong will only make these feelings worse, as if you've only got yourself to blame for your difficulties.

This simply isn't true. Core beliefs develop for very good reasons that make perfect sense at the time. Small children usually accept the ideas that are suggested to them by adults and by their culture, because they need to believe that the people caring for them are right and know best. And as we've already said they often work out their own ideas based on their life experience, so that some core beliefs arise because you need them at the time to get through a difficulty.

You can see for instance that a child who loses a parent might comfort themselves by thinking 'it's not my fault, all adults go away sooner or later', or they might take the exact opposite view and blame themselves – 'it's all my fault that they went away'.

The trouble is that the beliefs dig themselves in and hang on into adult life like bad habits that are hard to change. And yet they can be changed, with patience and determination. (Anyone who has reached this stage in the book can credit themselves with plenty of both.)

If you approach this with an open mind, and accept the possibility of change, you have every chance of success. You can't undo the past, but you can bring your adult mind to bear on the situation, and write new rules for yourself and test them out.

Examining your negative core beliefs

You have already started on the first step, which is identifying your negative core beliefs. This may take more than one try before you get to the heart of the matter – hitting on the key belief may be quite painful, or may bring a sense of relief as you recognise it for what it is. Once you have found a belief that seems to be important, examine how you feel about it at the moment. There are three possibilities:

1. You don't really believe it any more and you are ready to give it up.

2. Your head tells you it is wrong, but you continue to act as if it were true because of the emotional hold it has on you.

3. You still believe in it totally.

If you are ready to give the belief up, then doing the exercises below will help you reach that goal.

If you can still feel the emotional pull of a belief that you know is irrational, then you may have to work harder to shift it.

If you still believe in it totally then you will need to work even harder. The most important thing is that you want to shift it, and that you have the motivation to do so.

Challenging your negative core beliefs

Once you have identified your core beliefs, you can subject each one to a series of questions. Rather like putting Anxiety on trial, this is a way of shining a light onto it and understanding how it works.

Questions to ask:

Is this belief always true?

Does this belief have any benefit for me now?

Does this belief contribute to my well-being or my peace of mind?

Did I choose this belief myself as a way of surviving?

Did this belief come from the adults around me?

Example for someone whose core belief is 'I always fail'.

Is this belief always true? *No, I can think of times when I haven't failed, but they don't seem important.*

Does this belief have any benefit for me now? *It stops me getting bigheaded.*

Does this belief contribute to my well-being or my peace of mind? *It keeps me from taking on risky challenges because I know I'll fail at them.*

Did I choose this belief as a way of surviving? *Yes, because I was the youngest and I couldn't compete with the others.*

Did this belief come from the others around me? *No.*

Straight away you can see that the belief is not true all the time and that it only brings negative benefits – it stops the person from being adventurous. Above all you can see that it is no longer relevant to their adult life – they were the youngest, but they're not any more.

GROUP MEMBERS TALK ABOUT DEALING WITH THE PAST

'I don't look back at my childhood, I deal with the now – the past is gone.'
ANDREA

'I don't think my childhood gave me beliefs about the world that set me up for anxiety.'
ANDREW

'I learned depression as a child, it was a natural reaction to some very horrible things going on around me.'
BRIDGET

'In retrospect it is obvious to see a pattern emerging from my childhood experiences but I did not register this at the time.'
MARGARET

'My dad was a cautious chap. My mum was treated for nerves, it took a while before her doctors realised she was actually anaemic.'
PEN

'I didn't acquire negative beliefs about the world as a child – I used to be a daredevil.'
SARAH

'My mother left on several occasions, she found myself and three older sisters too stressful. Particularly as I was born when she was 44 and just beginning to get a bit of freedom, she was resentful of me.
I suspect dad was suffering from bi-polar. He became an alcoholic by the time I was 13 years old.'
TERESA

'We were a fairly relaxed family on the surface. My mother worried but she kept it all inside her, I never knew till later on when I was caring for her.'
WENDY

42 Changing Your Negative Core Beliefs

Changing negative core beliefs is a slow process but worth the effort. Some people cherish them as an essential part of themselves, but if something is making you unhappy, isn't it best to get rid of it?

One of the simplest techniques is also one of the most effective – countering. Once you have established your main negative core belief you can create a statement that counters it, and use it regularly. Write it in your diary, stick it to your bathroom mirror, remind yourself of it at every opportunity. Gradually the counter will come to seem more true than the original.

You could also record your counter statement and play it back regularly.

Another good technique is to work with another person and ask them to repeat your counter statement to you, while you return the favour and repeat their counter to them. (You don't have to find another Anxiety sufferer to work with, just someone who is also trying to make changes.)

Using counter statements for negative core beliefs

Examples

I'm powerless – *I can control my life.*

If I take a risk, I'll fail – *I can learn to take risks, step by step.*

If I fail, others will reject me – *I can cope with failure, and I can cope with rejection if it comes.*

I mustn't make mistakes – *I can learn from my mistakes.*

I'm not important – *I'm a worthwhile person.*

I should always look and behave in an acceptable way – *It's okay to be myself.*

If I worry enough things will get better – *action makes things better, not worrying.*

I can't cope with anything difficult or frightening – *I can do anything I set my mind to.*

The world is dangerous – *The danger in the world is manageable.*

I must stay within my comfort zone to keep safe – *I can create my own safe zone wherever I am.*

Be your own researcher

Treat yourself as a project and set out to discover as much about yourself as you can. Start with the negative core belief, for instance 'Nobody likes me'.

Then do research into the truth of this. You might look for evidence that you are liked – for instance:

- Are people generally pleased to see you?
- Are they pleased to hear your voice when you phone them up?
- Do they invite you to social events?

Evidence that you are not liked – for instance:

- Do people avoid you?
- Do people say unkind things to you?

You're likely to get some good surprises when you're researching your negative core beliefs. You'll find that some people do like you, and are astonished that you thought otherwise. There will always be some people that don't like aspects of your character, but that doesn't mean you're unlikeable as a person.

With a core belief such as 'I'm useless at everything' or 'I never get anything right' you could well find that other people see you quite differently – as competent and reliable for instance. While you may find this hard to believe, it will help you to chip away at that core belief.

You may also find that people are more aware of your Anxiety problem than you thought, and you may find this painful. Even those people who haven't been told about your problem may make remarks like 'we would ask you to our parties, but everyone knows you don't like parties'. In other words, they've misinterpreted the fact that you avoid socialising because of your Anxiety.

It's not only Anxiety sufferers who jump to conclusions, and you may hear remarks that you find quite hurtful, such as 'I know you don't like coming to my house because it's so small and scruffy'. At this point you have to choose whether to tell the person the real reason you don't visit them.

GROUP MEMBERS TALK

*'Think you **can** beat the bully of anxiety and you **will**. If you think you are beaten, then you are.'*
JULIE

'Anxiety neuroses are the most contrary and perverse illnesses to analyse. Coming to terms with the exaggerated and catastrophic thought processes and finding the way forward is not easy.'
MARGARET

'Before I became ill everything was okay. I had a good childhood. Nothing set me up for anxiety until the trauma happened.'
SARAH

'I realised how insecure I was. Feelings of inferiority and low self-esteem, which I largely attribute to my up bringing.'
TERESA

43 Summary of Work with Core Beliefs

There are any number of ways of describing what goes on inside a person's head, i.e. their thoughts, but the concept of three levels of thinking is a useful one when looking at Anxiety.

- The top layer is the thoughts that arise because of what is happening in the here and now. Many of these are automatic and arise so quickly that we are hardly aware of them.

- The middle layer consists of underlying assumptions which can be seen as a set of rules for living.

- The deepest layer is the core beliefs, the foundations upon which the middle level is built and which ultimately drive the whole process. In Anxiety sufferers these are often negative statements about your lack of self worth or your inability to cope.

If the three levels are all negative and Anxiety-focused then they will lock together to form a vicious circle.

All three types of thought can be challenged with counter statements. Your task is to identify your own negative thoughts, then compose a positive, affirming statement which contradicts the thought. The counter statement needs to be repeated over and over again until you find yourself automatically thinking the new positive thought every time the old negative one comes into your mind.

Also you can collect evidence to test the truth or otherwise of your beliefs. Negative beliefs are unlikely to represent the whole truth. Try to build up a more balanced picture by recording your own achievements and asking those around you for honest feedback.

> 'All that we are is the result of what we have thought. The mind is everything. What we think we become'.   Buddha

> 'There is nothing either good or bad, but thinking makes it so'.
>   Shakespeare, Hamlet

Part Four

44 Why Me?

Now you understand how Anxiety can change your thought processes, and how to start changing them back again. But at some point you will probably ask the question 'why me?' You may think something along the lines of 'look at Mrs Jones down the road, she's had plenty of stress and she doesn't panic'. Or you might read in the newspaper about people who come through terrible experiences and appear to be okay.

First of all, of course, you can't be absolutely sure about Mrs Jones or the people in the news – they may all have Anxiety problems that you don't know anything about. But quite possibly they don't, quite possibly they have managed to cope with difficulties without developing Anxiety. Why should this be? It may be that there are things going on in your mind, deeper aspects of your thoughts, that may have provided the foothold for Anxiety.

You already know that Anxiety is guilty, so now we're asking why you were targeted. It's like asking why did the burglar pick that house, or the mugger choose that victim?

Another question that is often asked is 'why has my Anxiety lasted so long?' Some people seem to have a short sharp experience of Anxiety that they quickly overcome, and yet other people suffer for months and years before they recover. Very often the same things that made you vulnerable to Anxiety are also the ones that keep your Anxiety going. They are known as maintenance factors.

So next we're going to look deeper into your thought processes, and at the aspects of your make up that might have made you vulnerable to Anxiety.

Understanding emotions

Your emotions are experienced in your brain, more specifically through a series of structures called the limbic system. This is part of your involuntary nervous system which as we've already seen also controls many bodily functions. Your emotions are influenced by your thoughts, and your perceptions, and they are expressed both through thoughts and through your body.

Simple emotions

Research suggests that there are six simple emotions that are found in all cultures, all over the world: happiness, anger, grief, sadness, fear, and disgust. Along with other simple emotions such as excitement, curiosity or boredom they are usually spontaneous and short-lived. They are your instant reaction to what is happening at that moment.

Complex emotions

Complex emotions are longer lasting and linked with your thought processes. They are also conditioned by your past experiences, especially as you were growing up – your family, your community, your wider culture all have a part to play. Examples of complex emotions are love, guilt, embarrassment and jealousy. You can see at once that they are affected by your experience of the world, so that people in different cultures would feel guilty or embarrassed about different things, and people from different families would show love in different ways.

Emotions are never right or wrong, they are a healthy and natural part of being human. They can be positive or negative, depending on the circumstances.

Your upbringing and early experiences may have caused you to believe that some emotions are not acceptable. If you were discouraged from expressing them you might, over time, reach a point of deliberately avoiding these feelings. This is repression, where a person has lost touch with some of their emotions.

Young children can be overwhelmed by strong emotions such as fear or anger. If no one reassures them and helps them to cope, then they don't learn how to move on from these emotions. This problem can carry on into adulthood, and a person can feel quite unable to manage the emotion in question, simply because they didn't learn to do so as a child.

Another aspect of this is the person who does not learn to contain their emotions and will be unable to tolerate any upset or frustration in their adult life. If hurt or upset they will cry, if angry they will be verbally or physically aggressive, if bored they will give up and walk away from whoever they are with or whatever they are doing. The fear of losing control forms the basis of their Anxiety, and they will avoid people and situations where they may be at risk of this.

Repression and anxiety

There seems to be a connection between repression and Anxiety, and anxious people often say that they find it hard to express their feelings, especially anger, grief and despair. The problem is that these feelings are there, and they are working away inside you like an untreated infection, causing difficulties that sooner or later will come to the surface.

Many anxious people have an underlying fear of losing control, even for a moment (which explains why some people find it so difficult to accept the need for relaxation). The fear is that loss of control will bring all of the withheld feelings bubbling to the surface.

Withheld feelings can be an underlying cause for all forms of Anxiety:

Panic

In some people panic attacks are a sign that their suppressed feelings of anger, grief or despair are trying to break through.

Phobias

Usually with a phobia the feared object is not in itself dangerous. Someone with a phobia of frogs knows full well that they are not dangerous and yet they still feel the fear. For some people the feared object is a symbol – it stands for their own feelings, and they are afraid of them.

Generalised anxiety disorder

It is well known that repressed feelings can contribute to physical problems such as headaches, ulcers and asthma, and in the same way repression can be a part of the free-floating Anxiety that is GAD.

OCD

If you monitor the times when your OCD is at its worst you're likely to find that it's when you feel frustrated, thwarted or angry with your situation in life.

In fact anger is the most common driver of Anxiety disorders. If someone feels trapped in an unsatisfactory life, or feels that they were cheated in the past (of education, career opportunities or the ability to be themselves for example) then their anger is likely to break out in the form of Anxiety.

GROUP MEMBERS TALK ABOUT FEELINGS

'I do tend to hold my feelings in.'
ANDREA

'I do most definitely hold my feelings in.'
ANDREW

'I don't hold my feelings in.'
BRIDGET

'I do hold my feelings in – with my stomach.'
PEN

'I used to hold my feelings in a lot of the time.'
SARAH

45 Dealing with Withheld Feelings

If you can learn to release your feelings instead of suppressing them you will find it helps the recovery process, and also helps stop the Anxiety from coming back once you have recovered. If you can deal with your feelings as they arise, you'll be more able to live in the present, and less bogged down in the past.

Although the process of releasing emotions can be painful at the time, afterwards people generally feel much better. The ancient Greeks knew all about this and they called it catharsis. Greek plays always aimed to send people home feeling better in this way – even a tragic play or film, while sad at the time, produces a feeling of release and catharsis afterwards.

The first step is to learn to recognise the feelings you are holding in. You may already be making progress towards that through the work you've already done.

- Regular relaxation puts you more in tune with your body, which helps you to recognise the physical sensations that are signs of deeper emotions.

- The cognitive work you've done so far will help you identify the emotions that are driving your thoughts.

In addition, you can keep a diary noting your emotional responses to events during the course of the day. Refer to the feelings list at the end of this section. Do any of yours seem inappropriate to the events which trigger them – too much or too little? Explore what this might mean. If there is a serious mismatch, for example, you become excessively angry over minor matters, or you do not react at all to a sad event, you might want to seek help from a counsellor.

Expressing your feelings

The next step is to learn to express your feelings. As usual it's best to aim to do this gradually, in small manageable steps. You can try:

Talking

Choose someone that you trust, who will listen to you without judging, criticising or offering advice. Also it needs to be someone who won't become upset if you cry or get angry. A professional counsellor, or a telephone helpline volunteer, will be able to do this, and their training will enable them to give you the kind of feedback that helps your journey of discovery. You can also talk to a good friend or family member.

Writing

Write your feelings out in a diary. Set aside a period of time each day for this and you'll gradually build up a picture of what's going on for you. You can also write a letter, either to yourself or to an imaginary person. If there is one person who is the focus for your feelings you can write it to them, (even if they are dead). Some people find it helps to destroy the letter once it's written, as a way of moving on from the emotions that fuelled it. Do not show the letter to the person – its function is to help you get your feelings out, and you need to express yourself freely. If you need to communicate your feelings to the person, then see 'Communicating', below.

Communicating

if your negative emotions are focused on someone around you, it is possible to communicate this to them. If you are upset or angry because of something they've said or done then the assertiveness techniques described in Chapter 46 will help you do this safely. However, if your problems go deeper into your relationship with them you'll have to proceed more carefully – we suggest you take professional advice (see Relate in Appendix 2).

Unblocking

If you find it hard to release your feelings you can unblock them – for instance, watching a sad TV programme or a film can help you to cry. Choose something that you know you'll enjoy watching despite the sadness, such as your favourite soap, or a film on DVD. Music also has a powerful emotional effect for many of us and will help you to release your feelings.

Physical action

This is particularly good for releasing anger. Find a way that won't hurt you, or anyone else, or damage anything. You can thump a cushion, throw a ball hard against a wall, yell and shout, or take vigorous exercise.

Identifying your negative emotions

Use the checklist below to identify which negative emotions you need to release:

- ☐ Aggression
- ☐ Annoyance
- ☐ Contempt
- ☐ Disappointment
- ☐ Envy
- ☐ Embarrassment
- ☐ Frustration
- ☐ Grief
- ☐ Guilt
- ☐ Hatred
- ☐ Jealousy
- ☐ Loneliness

☐ Rage
☐ Regret
☐ Remorse
☐ Shame

Decide which of the techniques is best for you, for each of the emotions.

☐ Writing
☐ Unblocking
☐ Physical action
☐ Communicating

Tackle the work of releasing your emotions in small manageable steps. Allow plenty of time for it.

People who have problems with controlling their emotional responses can use some of the same methods to discharge their feelings safely, then work on strengthening their adult coping mechanisms through assertiveness training (see Chapter 46).

GROUP MEMBERS TALK ABOUT BECOMING OPEN TO FEELINGS

'I've tried to change, it comes with assertiveness I think.'
ANDREW

'I am learning to exteriorise myself but I still hold a lot in, because I have trouble trusting people. However I'm comfortable with this and don't plan to make much change in the future.'
JULIE

'I haven't come to terms with that one at all, it goes back to childhood. I hate crying.'
PEN

'Also to talk through my feelings I do find that talking through every thing that's going on in my head with somebody I trust helps me loads.'
SARAH

'I do let my feelings out to certain people, it depends on the person and how close they are to me.'
WENDY

46 Assertiveness

Assertiveness means being able to both meet your own needs and acknowledge the needs of other people. It's not about always getting your own way, or getting other people to do what you want. It means acting in a confident, adult way to get what you need, or to resist unreasonable demands. It doesn't mean acting in ways that are aggressive, bullying, threatening or manipulative.

An assertive person knows that they have certain rights. The most important ones are:

- The right to ask for what you need.
- The right to say 'No' without feeling guilty.
- The right to your opinions.
- The right to your feelings.

Of course other people have the same rights, so assertiveness is about being fair. It often means looking for a compromise solution, where you can have what you need without depriving someone else – known as a win-win solution.

You lack assertiveness if you:

- Feel unable to speak up.
- Often feel ignored.
- Resent the way other people treat you.
- Can't cope with aggression or anger in other people.

- Will do anything for a quiet life.
- Say 'yes' when you mean 'no'.

Assertiveness and anxiety

Many Anxiety sufferers find it difficult to be assertive, and tend to act submissively. They are afraid to speak up for themselves, or state their needs openly. It can be especially difficult to be assertive if you are dependant on another person for care and support, and yet lack of assertiveness can breed feelings of resentment that only fuel your Anxiety.

One of the most important skills in assertiveness is communicating your needs, and your feelings, to other people. For instance, do you find it hard to tell someone that you're upset or angry because of something they've said or done? It certainly is a risky thing to do, and it needs to be done carefully and in a way which respects the other person's feelings.

You may not always achieve the outcome you would like in the short-term, but as you develop the habit of communicating assertively, other people will start to treat you with more respect. Before you undertake this kind of communication, spend some time thinking about what you are going to say. You can also rehearse it in role-playing sessions with a counsellor or helper.

Developing assertive communication

Here are some basic rules for this type of communication:

1. Choose an appropriate time.

2. Take responsibility for your feelings.

3. Refer to specific behaviours rather than making sweeping statements.

Let's take the example of someone who feels aggrieved at the way the whole family rely on them to act as an unpaid chauffeur. First, how they handle this in a non-assertive way:

1. Start complaining when a family member is ready to leave the house and reminds the person that they need a lift.

2. Say to the family member 'you make me so cross the way you expect lifts all the time'.

3. Say 'you're all the same, none of you thinks about me at all'.

This might seem like perfectly normal behaviour, indeed it is for many of us, but I'm sure you can imagine how it ends – the family member responds with anger, storms out of the house and both of them sulk in the car. An assertive communication might be more like this:

1. Choose a time when things are fairly calm, and there is time to talk.

2. Say 'I feel cross when you keep asking me for lifts'.

3. Say 'I realise you need the lift, but I need a break in the evenings, so how about if you get the bus?'

Another useful skill is boundary setting. This simply means being clear about what you will, and will not do. Once you have set a boundary, communicate it clearly and stick to it. In the lift example the person might set boundaries in this way:

1. Choose a time when things are fairly calm, and there is time to talk.

2. Say 'I won't be able to give anyone a lift on Tuesday evenings, that's going to be my evening off'.

3. Stick to the boundary once you've set it.

GROUP MEMBERS TALK ABOUT ASSERTIVENESS

'I don't find it difficult to be assertive.'
ANDREA

'I do find it difficult to be assertive, but I've improved over the years. With maturity you develop a different approach to life and things don't bother you as much – things like making a good impression.'
ANDREW

'I don't find it difficult to be assertive, although I don't always confront issues, because I worry about being too assertive.'
BRIDGET

'I used to find it very difficult to be assertive, but I have changed that now.'
JULIE

'I sometimes find it difficult to be assertive. Even as a teacher I wasn't assertive. I don't like having to negotiate to get what I see as my right.'
PEN

'I do find it difficult to be assertive – it's hard for me to say "no".'
SARAH

'I have searched for guidance in the form of confidence and assertiveness classes.'
TERESA

'I used to find it difficult to be assertive but not now. Before if somebody said something I either left the room or lost my temper. Now I can talk it through.'
WENDY

47 Self-confidence and Self-esteem

Lack of self-confidence and low self-esteem are other maintenance factors for Anxiety. Anxiety can strike both the confident and unconfident, but almost always it has the effect of destroying whatever self-confidence the person had.

Repeatedly avoiding social situations, spending hours locked into rituals, making Anxiety behaviours the most important thing in your life, will all have the effect of cutting you off from normal life and reducing self-confidence. Being dependant on other people to manage your life and your Anxiety also affects your self-confidence.

For some people the lack of confidence goes deeper than the Anxiety, into a fundamental part of their make up. It will affect relationships, lead to chronic stress and may be connected to past traumas that still need resolving.

For these people it's not just a question of confidence, but of self-esteem. Low self-esteem is about failing to accept yourself as you are, and failing to have respect for yourself. This starts in childhood and can come from:

- parents who are too critical
- significant loss (for example of a parent) during childhood
- physical or sexual abuse
- neglect
- rejection
- parents who are too protective
- parents who are too indulgent.

A person with low self-esteem will find it difficult to love and nurture themselves and won't be able to care for their own needs. The demands and responsibilities of adult life will overwhelm them, and Anxiety is the result.

This is a very common difficulty for all Anxiety sufferers, but especially for agoraphobics and social phobics who tend to set a lot of store by other people's opinions.

Building confidence and self-esteem

All of the work you have already done will help you build your self-confidence, in particular:

- Improving physical fitness.
- Finding the motivation for a recovery programme.
- Understanding how Anxiety works.
- Achieving successes in exposure work.
- Countering negative self-talk.

You could also try:

- Giving yourself a makeover.
- Asking for positive feedback from supportive people.
- Creating an activity diary – plan activities that are more satisfying to you.
- Volunteering to help with a local charity or project.

Many people find that volunteering provides a useful step on the road to recovery. It's important to wait until you are well enough, so that you have some spare time and energy, but at that point doing something for others is a great way to build your self-esteem and self-confidence. There is a huge range of volunteering opportunities, so you should be able to find something that interests you, and that fits in with any restrictions that Anxiety still imposes on you.

Healing your inner child

The idea that each one of us has an inner child has been the butt of jokes in recent years, and yet it's a concept that is useful in understanding ourselves. We all still have, inside us, the child that we used to be – spontaneous, creative, playful, fearful and insecure.

Children experience life in a very direct way, and without depth of understanding, and childhood experiences stay with us in ways that can be hard to put into words.

In many ways Anxiety takes us back to childhood, and anxious fears often have the same irrational nightmarish quality of childhood fears. Recovery consists of gently taking yourself back into the adult world.

If you experienced trauma as a child and you haven't been able to deal with it, then you will still be carrying the pain of it and that may well be feeding into your Anxiety. This can be healed but self-help may not be sufficient, especially for working on experiences which occurred very early in your life, before you had developed language or thought capacity to understand what was happening. If this is the case for you, we recommend that you look for professional help from a counsellor or psychotherapist.

GROUP MEMBERS TALK ABOUT SELF-ESTEEM

'My self-esteem has certainly been low in the past – my stammer lasted till I was 25 and even now I worry on the bus about asking for the fare.'
ANDREW

'My self esteem is fine.'
BRIDGET

'I also had very low self-esteem, and I've had to work on that.'
JULIE

'As for self-esteem, I'm told that I always doubt my ability and I don't praise myself for my achievements, even though I know I've achieved a lot.'
PEN

'I do put myself down, don't like myself, laugh at myself. But I am better than a lot of people I know – many in the hospital were worse than me. The feeling of doing something good for those less fortunate gives me an amazing feeling which gives me something to focus on when "Life is rubbish and I want to die".'
SARAH

'My self-esteem was very low, but everything turned round when my mum went into a Home.'
WENDY

48 Problems and Decisions

Finding new ways of looking at your problems and dealing with them is a running theme through this book and you will have realised by now that the tools and techniques of self-help can be adapted to many situations. Goal-setting and using small steps along the way are particularly useful skills to help you work your way through complicated problems.

Anxiety clogs up your thought processes, and you can find yourself going round the same old loop as you try to solve a problem or make a decision. Negative thinking and the ability to keep generating 'what if' thoughts in particular can lead to you feeling frozen and unable to move forward to a solution or a decision.

Emotional reasoning can also be a barrier to good decision making. There are some things that just can't be resolved by answering the question 'do I *feel* like it?' and others that need many more factors to be taken into consideration.

Even a simple decision can have more than one aspect. If someone says 'I'm just making a hot drink, do you want one?', the first thing you'll ask yourself is 'am I thirsty?' But even if you are not thirsty you might still say yes to the drink because you fancy a break from what you're doing, or you'd relish the chance to sit down and chat with the other person.

If you make the wrong decision about a hot drink it won't really matter, but some decisions need more thought. The first step is just to allocate a level of importance to the decision. Deciding about the drink is very unimportant – you could give that 1 out of 10 – whereas deciding which house to buy is, for most of us, very important – 9 out of 10 say.

Anxiety and negative thinking can cause you to lose your sense of perspective and allow small things to become too important, so this is a very useful step that will stop you worrying needlessly about small things.

Decision making

If the decision is important enough to warrant some effort, a points system is a good way of proceeding. Start by making a list of all the important aspects of the decision. Just doing this will clarify your thoughts and may in itself make it clear what you want to do. You can include both emotional and practical items.

Here is an example of one list for a family trying to decide whether to have a camping holiday in the UK or a package holiday in Spain. The items on their list are: cheapness, travel, weather, accommodation, adventure, beach.

The next step is to give points out of 10 for each of the items on the list for the two holidays, as follows:

	Camping	Spain
Cheapness	9	4
Travel	8	2
Weather	3	9
Accommodation	2	7
Adventure	7	4
Beach	5	9
TOTAL	34	35

At this point there isn't much to choose between them. However, not all the factors are of equal importance, and you can reflect this by weighting each item. This just means increasing the score of important items by multiplying them by a chosen number.

In our example, the family really need a cheap holiday so they multiply the cheapness score by 3.

	Camping	Spain
Cheapness	**27**	**12**
Travel	8	2
Weather	3	9
Accommodation	2	7
Adventure	7	4
Beach	5	9
TOTAL	52	43

Now a gap emerges, and Camping starts to look like the best option.

And what happens if you work through this process and are dismayed to find that the wrong item has the highest score? That just means that you knew all along what you wanted to do!

Problem solving

Of course there are other ways of making decisions, all that matters is to find one that works for you and stops you getting bogged down in anxious thoughts. And the system described has the advantage of clarity.

Clarity is also needed in problem solving – before you can solve a problem you have to know just what the problem is. The basic steps in problem solving are:

1. Establish what the problem is.
2. Establish how important it is.
3. Establish how urgent it is.
4. Look at possible solutions.
5. Choose the best solution.
6. Implement the solution.

Let's work through a version of the holiday example above.

1. What is the problem? *Some family members want a camping holiday in the UK, others want a package holiday in Spain.*

2. How important is it? *Very important – with both parents working, family time together is precious and needs to be right.*

3. How urgent is it? *Pretty urgent, since they've left it late to sort this out.*

4. What are the possible solutions? The obvious solutions are:
    Go camping in the UK.
    Go to Spain.
    Do one this year, and the other next year.

However some lateral thinking produces other possibilities:
    Do something else that everyone agrees on.
    Go camping in Spain.
    Go on a package-type holiday in the UK.

This stage is absolutely crucial and shows the advantage of free and open discussion. When everybody is encouraged to speak up then ideas soon start to flow. In this case the idea of camping on a site in Spain with plenty of activities suited everybody and from that point it was easy to Choose and Implement the best solution.

49 The Meaning of Life

If your Anxiety has lasted a long time, and if you feel that however hard you try you simply can't make progress with your recovery, then it may help to look at your whole life. What were you doing before Anxiety struck? Were you happy and fulfilled? If the answers are that you were doing something you disliked, and you weren't especially happy or fulfilled, then clearly you'll have no desire to return to that life.

This is why it can sometimes seem that an Anxiety sufferer gets some benefit from their illness. If you can get someone else to do the tiresome chores, if you never have to be the one that's responsible, if you can cut out having to deal with office politics, dead-end jobs and relationship issues, then you might secretly feel that Anxiety has some advantages. Of course the gains are nothing compared with the losses, but if you can't see any point at all in re-engaging with life then you will find it hard to develop the motivation for recovery.

Even people who have made good progress in their recovery sometimes feel disappointed in what their new life has to offer them.

In other words, some people find that recovery ultimately depends on finding a broad purpose or direction to give their life greater meaning. This may involve developing an unused talent or skill – boredom from unused potential can be a breeding ground for Anxiety. It may mean achieving peace of mind through a connection with a spiritual force, through a religious faith or philosophy, or working to make a difference in the world through political or social action.

Another, connected problem occurs when people feel trapped in a situation that they can't manage in ways that suit them. This could be a relationship or a job that makes demands or imposes structures that they just can't cope with. Anxiety takes them away from it, and however hard they work at recovery they will always have a secret fear of dealing with it.

Are you resisting recovery?

These are very difficult issues for any Anxiety sufferer to face directly, because it can feel as if they're being accused of doing it deliberately, of making themselves ill just to get out of chores or an awkward situation.

You didn't deliberately make yourself ill with Anxiety. Nobody does. Do, however, think carefully about what we've said. Ask yourself if there is something about the prospect of a life without Anxiety that daunts you, scares you or simply bores you.

If you're finding it difficult to explore this idea, try this visualisation exercise to help you:

- Lie down or sit comfortably.

- Take a few moments to relax yourself.

- Imagine yourself doing something that you haven't been able to do for a while.

- Picture the whole scene, with you in it, behaving calmly and without Anxiety.

- What is good about the scene?

- What is bad about the scene?

Repeat this exercise for different scenarios until you come across one, or more, where you find it difficult to imagine being happy with the situation.

224

Sometimes resistance to recovery comes from your core beliefs. You may believe deep down that you are not meant to succeed. Or an 'all-or nothing' belief leads you to view anything less than 100% recovery as a failure. If this is the case, when you meet an obstacle of any kind, the old thought-pattern will assert itself, and you will interpret this as a major set-back. Remember that plateaux and set-backs are to be expected, and you can get through them. If you find it hard to shift these entrenched beliefs on your own, use your support system to do more work on your thinking.

This is also something that a trained counsellor can help you to explore if you're finding it difficult to do on your own.

Facing up to difficult issues

Once you have worked out what it is that you find difficult to face, you can decide if there's anything that can be done about it. Sometimes it's a question of using assertiveness or problem solving skills to manage your life in a different way. Learning to say 'No', encouraging people to treat you differently and setting boundaries can all help you make big changes in your life.

Sometimes, however, there may be larger issues to face. If your work is deeply unsatisfying to you then you may need to consider retraining for something that you are more suited to. This may not be easy if there are bills to pay while you retrain, or if your preferred work doesn't pay as well as your current work.

Similarly, you may find yourself facing great difficulties in a relationship. It may even be that you will have to move on from a relationship, with all the upheaval and emotional turmoil involved.

These things are not easy, and for some people retreat into Anxiety can seem like their best option. If this is the case for you, consider getting professional help.

GROUP MEMBERS TALK ABOUT ENCOURAGEMENT

'The road to recovery seems to stretch for miles and involve many twists, turns and side turnings. It is also very bumpy and yes, painful too. It requires a lot of commitments and hard work on your part and has to be walked on one step at a time.'
JULIE

'... the extraordinary bravery that some people have shown when faced with almost unbelievable and complicated problems.'
MARGARET

'I try to make myself do things, socialise in spite of feeling anxious. But I avoid the places associated with the rapist. As he lives in the area where my mates are, it is difficult for me not to become isolated.'
SARAH

'I had group therapy at the same time as relate counselling (which I attended on my own). This opened my eyes to the way I looked at life. My coping strategies, or lack of them. I have since completed a level 3 counselling course.'
TERESA

50 Dealing with Maintenance Factors – Summary

As you can see maintenance factors are all about the kind of person you are apart from your Anxiety, and the kind of life you were living before Anxiety struck. Making changes in these areas is difficult for anybody, and may well require the kind of energy you simply don't have while your Anxiety is at its worst.

But once you have made some progress towards recovery you will free up some of the energy that was going into your Anxiety and you can start to think about making changes at this next level.

If you feel daunted by this, then consider moving beyond self-help. You can explore withheld feelings, lack of confidence, low self esteem and damaged inner child with a counsellor or therapist. If you choose a person-centred counsellor then you can be sure that you will stay in control of how far you go with this work.

Assertiveness, problem solving and decision making can all be learnt on courses – check out what evening classes and other courses are available to you locally.

If you need to explore your spiritual side don't be afraid to turn to the religious leaders in your local community.

Checklist for maintenance factors

Use this checklist to make sure you've considered all of the possible maintenance factors for your Anxiety.

- ☐ Why me?
- ☐ Emotions, mind/body, repression
- ☐ Assertiveness
- ☐ Confidence and self-esteem
- ☐ Healing your inner child
- ☐ Problem solving and decision making
- ☐ The meaning of life
- ☐ Resisting recovery
- ☐ Difficult issues

GROUP MEMBERS TALK – WORDS OF WISDOM

'My advice to anyone recovering from tranquilliser withdrawal is – do it slowly. Even if it's a tough journey, you can do it. My advice for anyone with General Anxiety is – use positive thinking, and alleviate your anxiety by living well and looking after yourself.'
ANDREA

'The best advice I can give to anyone who thinks they have tried everything and nothing has worked is: be prepared to go round the loop again. Maybe something wasn't right for you at the time, but later on you might be ready for it.'
ANDREW

'I know that you can . . . use your life experiences to teach yourself to be happy. I can feel joy as well as sadness.'
BRIDGET

'Just like the mountain climber has tools to help him on his way, you have your positive thinking, breathing exercises and relaxation techniques to help you through it. Keeping a diary and recording your stress level along the way is also a fine idea, just like setting yourself small gradual goals to take it one step at a time.'
JULIE

'We cannot change our past but we can learn from it.'
MARGARET

> *'So the choice is yours, control is at hand.*
> *Don't suffer for life as it can be made grand.*
> *This thing can be conquered, it's not just for the few.*
> *If you control this illness then it can't control you.'*

NORMAN

'I'd advise anyone starting on recovery to look to breathing and relaxation to bring it under control. There is no instant fix and you can expect setbacks and plateaux. Find out what works for you and stick at it, don't ease off on the practising when you start to feel better.'
PEN

'My advice for people about to start on recovery from anxiety is get a healthy diet, take exercise, make sure you know what your needs are and how to get them met. Also keep occupied – have something in place for when you feel anxious, so that you won't do something which feeds the anxiety.'
SARAH

'I think parenting classes was one of the breakthroughs, of realising how I was making the same mistakes as my parents.'
TERESA

'It takes blood sweat and tears, and a lot of tears – but tears are alright, if you cry you're getting it out of your system.'
WENDY

51 Finale

So you've reached the end of the book – or maybe you're having a quick peek at the end to see where the journey leads, or have skimmed through, dipping in and out. We've designed this book to be used as a complete programme, taking things in the order that we believe will help you get the best from it, but we know that very few people read self-help books like that, to start with at any rate.

If you've been skimming, dipping, or jumped straight to the end, then we suggest you take a deep breath and set about working through the chapters from the beginning, giving each task your full attention, and taking as much time as you need.

Once you've done that, you can assess the progress you've made. You will, for sure, have learnt much about yourself, and about Anxiety. You may have been able to use that knowledge, and the techniques we describe, to start on the road to a life free from Anxiety (no one will ever be entirely free from normal anxiety). You may even feel that you have travelled so far along that road that you consider yourself to have recovered from Anxiety.

But the story isn't finished yet.

How are you feeling?

While you are in the grip of an Anxiety disorder it's easy to think that life would be wonderful and simple if only you weren't so anxious. In fact as you move through recovery you're likely to feel complicated emotions, some of which may take you by surprise. Spend some time thinking about this, and make a list of the emotions you're feeling. Here are some likely candidates:

- Elation – that wonderful moment when you manage a task.
- Excitement – you have a whole new life.
- Pride – at your achievements so far.
- Disappointment – if you haven't come as far as you wanted.
- Apprehension – what does the future hold?
- Sadness – you are leaving your old life behind.
- Worry – what if my Anxiety comes back?

If you are elated, excited or proud then just enjoy the moment. Don't, whatever you do, belittle your achievements. If you've managed something that was difficult for you then you deserve to feel happy about it.

What about if you're disappointed? Take a moment to look through your notebook – it will remind you of how far you've come and how much more you now understand about Anxiety. Remember that everyone has different needs and will move at a different pace. You can go through any part of the programme again, or all of it. Before you do, ask yourself if you need to set new goals, and if they need to be more realistic.

If you're apprehensive about the future, give yourself time to adapt to a life without Anxiety. All Anxiety disorders absorb a lot of your time and energy, and tend to make you isolated. As you come out of Anxiety's confining world you may find that things have changed in ways that confuse you at first. Don't worry about it, and use your new skills to tackle things one at a time. After all, someone who has been in hospital for a while, or who has been living abroad, would have to cope with the same changes.

You might feel surprised that sadness was on the list, and yet this is a normal part of change. If there is a new beginning, then there must have been an ending. If there is a gain, there will always have been a loss.

If you suffered from Anxiety for a long time, then you will have made little adjustments that made life more bearable. The weekly visit from the person who kindly did your shopping may have been a highlight in a life with no social contact, but now you do your own shopping and you don't need them any more.

Also you may feel sad at the number of tedious things you are now able to do. Shopping for clothes may be fun, but shopping for soap and frozen peas is just a chore for most of us. Anxiety has let you off that particular hook.

These feelings are a normal part of letting go of old patterns. Don't try to block these feelings out, tell yourself that they will pass, and that every life has some light and shade in it. And you do have to let go of the old, so that there is room for the new opportunities that await you.

If you are worried about your Anxiety returning, that's understandable, but you now have new insight and new skills. Instead of dreading the bolt from the blue, you can now look back and see how your Anxiety developed in the first place.

You can identify the little warning signs that you ignored the first time around. If you get those signs again, you'll recognise them and, even better, you'll know what to do. Out of all the different things we've suggested you'll know by now which are the most helpful for you personally. If you feel yourself slipping back into Anxiety, then take action to stop the slide. Put things in place that you know are helpful – dig out your relaxation CD, check your eating habits, remember to be assertive and challenge your thoughts. In other words, take care of yourself.

And remember that recovery does not always progress in a straight line. It can also be viewed as a cycle. You may need to go round more than once, but you can keep coming back, and each time it will get easier.

GROUP MEMBERS TALK ABOUT RECOVERY

'Now I can do everything I want to do.'
JULIE

'From what you hear about OCD.
It sounds so terrible, but it need not be.
They say that it's chronic, and you've got it for life.
But the keyword's control, which can end all this strife.

If you give in to a bully then they'll keep coming back.
So why let them do it, face up to the flack
It's the same with this illness, it wants to control you.
Don't give it the pleasure! You can face life anew.

If your guard is dropped then it might just return.
But this thing doesn't always have to sting and burn.
Laugh at it, face it, don't let it win.
Be in control, it's not that great a sin.'

NORMAN

'I am making progress but I could wish it was faster.'
PEN

'I'm learning to drive. I do voluntary work and am going to build this
up to full time, as preparation for getting a job eventually.'
SARAH

'I'm a No Panic help line volunteer and mentor for other sufferers.'
WENDY

Hammersmith Library

User name: Khademi,
Marzeyah (Miss)
User ID: 2800500585487

Library name:
Hammersmith Library

Title: Free yourself from
anxiety : a self-help guide
to
Item ID: 38005013276550
Date due: 22/8/2019,23:59

Thank You
Hammersmith & Fulham
Libraries
http://www.lbhf.gov.uk
More than a library!

52 It's Okay to be Me

How will you know when you've done enough work on your recovery? It depends what you're aiming for, but feeling comfortable in your own skin is a good place to be. It's so easy for children to develop low self-esteem, and to feel that they don't measure up, because they are being assessed all the time, at home, at school and even in their leisure activities. Adults learn to let go of this mentality and accept themselves as they are.

If you continue with your healthy lifestyle, and your positive thinking, continue to be more assertive in dealing with other people and continue to release feelings instead of bottling them up, then you will change in ways that you would not have thought possible. The changes in your everyday life will be permanent and at a deep level – things will happen, but you'll take them in your stride instead of using them as yet another chance to judge yourself.

Working on your self-esteem can be a long and painful process but it is essential as part of learning to be okay with who you are. You may have to contend with some deep-rooted beliefs about not being of value, or of not deserving a good life, or of needing to conform.

Remember that adults don't need to prove themselves by their achievements. Life is not a test which we pass or fail. If you can free yourself from the authority figures of your childhood, and free yourself from the need to please them, then you will acquire the freedom to be yourself. You will no longer fear other people's disapproval.

You also don't need to feel guilty about the journey you are on. Of course it's true that many people alive today do not have the luxury of worrying about their self-esteem, or their core beliefs, because they are entirely focused on survival – enough to eat, a future for their children.

But don't say to yourself 'I'm feeble because I'm struggling with issues that so many people can never have the chance to think about'. You are not feeble, although you may be lucky that your basic needs are taken care of.

It seems to be the case with all human beings that once we have managed those basic human needs (food, water, air, sleep) we then turn our attention to other matters. Even the most primitive of human cultures have a spiritual aspect, and allow their priests or shamans to live without working the land or hunting. All you are doing is moving away from the basic survival needs to the deeper needs that we all have.

As you let go of Anxiety and learn to relish your new life you will probably become aware that you have unused potential. You may decide to explore your creativity, learn a new skill or widen your social network. When you open yourself to life, new opportunities seem to arise almost magically.

Further help

If you feel you've done as much as you can through self-help, and want to make still more progress, then you can look elsewhere for help and support. Sometimes all that is needed is a little input from someone who understands, and there are charities that offer mentoring schemes for people with Anxiety disorders. Or you may decide to speak to a counsellor or psychotherapist – this is especially useful if you have identified difficulties in your past that you need to address.

There are many types of counselling and psychotherapy. Some types are more suited to short-term work, with a fixed number of sessions. In fact cognitive behavioural therapy is typically delivered in between six and 15 sessions.

If you need to explore issues of self-development or personal growth, or to overcome the effects of childhood deprivation or abuse, you are likely to need a longer and more open-ended approach.

The main types of open-ended help are:

- Psychodynamic – based on the ideas of Sigmund Freud.
- Humanistic – including person-centred counselling, gestalt therapy and many others.

Some practitioners describe themselves as 'integrative'. This means their training has covered more than one approach, and they can choose between the different styles to suit each individual client. Sometimes you will see the word 'holistic' applied to therapy. A holistic practitioner claims to treat the whole person, to look at the cause of their illness as well as the symptoms, and to examine all aspects of the problem (mental, physical, spiritual and emotional).

Do choose someone who is registered with the United Kingdom Register of Counsellors (UKRC). This means that the counsellor must be appropriately trained and qualified, work to a Code of Ethics & Practice and be subject to a complaints procedure. To get details of registered counsellors in your area, contact the British Association for Counselling and Psychotherapy.

Goodbye to the group

It's time to say goodbye to Andrea, Andrew, Bridget, Julie, Margaret, Norman, Pen, Sarah, Teresa and Wendy. By reading their stories we hope you can see that Anxiety is an illness that strikes ordinary people. If you have an Anxiety disorder you are not odd or strange, and above all you are not alone. You are part of a large group of people, none of whom chose to join the group.

You can also see from their stories that recovery is possible and that life can feel good again. All of them have travelled from mental anguish to a position where, at the very least, they feel optimistic about the future. Some of them are already fully recovered, and some of them are able to help others by working as volunteers with one of the charities in the field. Their generosity in telling their stories, and reliving some of their pain, shows how much they want to help.

Extra Information

1. Script for muscle relaxation

This simple relaxation exercise teaches you to tense each set of muscles in turn and then relax it. As you work your way around your body you will gradually become more relaxed.

You can use this script by reading to yourself or by recording it and playing it back. You can also ask someone else to read it to you or record it. Be sure to read it slowly, in a calm voice, and pause for several seconds at the end of each section.

Very few people become fully relaxed the first time they try – it often takes many repetitions, and each time you work through a relaxation session you will gain a little more benefit – it builds up slowly. Occasionally the first session has the opposite effect, and it sends you into a deep sleep. Don't be concerned if this happens to you, it's only a sign that anxiety was making you very tired.

Remember to relax in a place that is warm, safe and comfortable. Arrange things so that you won't be disturbed for the half hour or so that it takes. Sit comfortably or lie down to do your relaxation. Where the script says 'hold it', you should maintain the tension in that muscle for a few seconds.

Script

Focus on the word relax. Breathe in and out through your nose and let your breathing slow down. Each time you breathe out, let yourself relax a little more. Close your eyes, and focus on the word relax.

Clench your fists. Feel the tension in your fists. Hold it. Relax your fists and let yourself feel the difference as your hands relax. Breathe quietly, and focus on the word relax.

Now bend your arms at the elbows. Try to bring your wrists right up to your shoulders. Hold it and feel the tension in your upper arms. Relax your arms and let them fall back comfortably. Let yourself feel the difference as your arms relax. Keep focusing on the word relax.

Straighten your arms as hard as you can. Hold it and feel the tension in the backs of your arms. Relax your arms and notice the difference in your muscles.

Shrug your shoulders, bringing them up towards your ears. Hold it. Feel the tension in your shoulders. Relax and feel the difference.

Press your head back, hard. Harder. Hold it and feel the tension in your neck. Really feel it. Now relax and feel the difference.

Raise your eyebrows and wrinkle up your forehead. Hold it and feel the tension in your forehead. Now relax your eyebrows and forehead. Keep breathing slowly and calmly.

Now frown and squeeze your eyelids tightly shut. Feel the tension in your eyelids as you hold it. Relax and feel the difference.

Clench your teeth as tightly as you can. Really feel your jaw muscles tighten up. Hold it, then relax and feel the difference. Focus on the word relax.

Next, push your tongue up against the roof of your mouth. Hold it and feel the tension inside your mouth and throat. Relax your tongue and feel the difference.

Press your lips tightly together. Hold it and really squeeze your lips together. Relax and feel the difference.

Tense your chest muscles by taking a deep breath. Hold it, then relax by breathing out. Feel the difference as your chest muscles relax. Let your breathing be slow and calm again.

Now clench your stomach muscles tightly. Hold it and clench your stomach muscles as tightly as you can. Relax, and feel the difference.

Arch your back slightly and clench your buttocks. Hold it and feel the tension in your back and buttocks. Relax, and feel the difference. Focus on the word relax, and breathe gently and calmly.

Straighten your legs, and point your toes downwards. Hold it and feel the tension in your legs and feet. Relax, and feel the difference. Keep focusing on the word relax.

Let the feelings of relaxation spread throughout your body. Feel every muscle return to a position of relaxation. Allow yourself to enjoy the peaceful calm feeling of relaxation. Stay quietly relaxed for a few more minutes. When you are ready, stand up slowly.

2. Breathing

More about breathing – physical
Your lungs are inside your ribcage, and there is a whole network of muscles that help you with the movements that will expand and contract your lungs. Healthy breathing uses all of these muscles.

Imagine your lungs have three sections – top, middle and bottom. Unhealthy breathing, as you already know, only uses the top section. Here's how to feel each of the three sections:

1. Sit or stand, keeping your back straight. Relax.

2. Lift your shoulders towards your ears and breathe in. Breathe out. Relax.

3. Push out your chest and ribs and breathe in. Breathe out. Relax.

4. Push down and out with your stomach, just above your navel and breathe in. Breathe out. Relax.

Take your time with this exercise. Only do as much as you feel able to do – if you have been breathing badly for years, you might find it quite strange to breathe correctly. The final stage, where you push your stomach out as you breathe in, is actually using your diaphragm, a strong muscle that sits underneath your lungs.

Once you're comfortable with the three sections, you can learn how to breathe smoothly through all of them.

1. Sit or stand, keeping your back straight. Relax.

2. Breathe in smoothly, raise your stomach up and out, open up your chest and ribs, and finally lift your shoulders just a little.

3. Breathe out smoothly, letting your shoulders fall, your ribs sink back and pulling your stomach in. Finish by pushing your stomach up a little to push out the last of the stale air.

As you can see, this is quite complicated and takes a while to master. Practise it every day, say for two sessions of 15 minutes each. Because it is complicated you will find that you are breathing much more slowly, and that is a good thing. Aim to breathe in and out about eight times a minute – you might find this difficult at first, but persevere.

More about breathing – emotional

There is a strong connection between breathing and your emotional state.

Excitement can make you feel breathless, distress can make you sob, emotional pain can make you hold your breath and so on. It's a two-way street, and changing your breathing can bring about a change in your emotions.

More breathing exercises

Here are some alternative ways of working with your breathing and calming yourself, taken from Yoga.

The divided breath

This breathing exercise is calming, and also some people find it helps them to fall asleep. It also exercises your diaphragm and makes it stronger.

1. Stand, sit or lie comfortably.

2. Breathe in slowly, smoothly and fully.

3. Breathe out in stages, with a short pause between each one – use two, three or four stages.

4. On the last stage don't force the air out of your lungs, but breathe out gently till you feel your stomach muscles tighten slightly.

5. Breathe in slowly, smoothly and fully.

The sniffing breath

The sniffing breath is a way of freeing up a tight chest.

1. Stand, sit or lie comfortably.

2. Breathe in in two or more quick sniffs.

3. Breathe out slowly.

4. Repeat two and three several times until you feel your chest relax.

5. Breathe normally.

The candle breath

This helps with diaphragm control and relaxation. You will need a lighted candle – be careful with it.

1. Sit comfortably in front of the candle.

2. Breathe in slowly through your nose.

3. Breathe out gently through your mouth – make the flame flicker, but do not blow it out.

4. Repeat several times.

5. If you become tired, take a rest.

3. Coming off tranquillisers and anti-depressants

If you have been prescribed drugs for Anxiety, especially if you have been taking them for some time, you may wish to give them up. This may be because you think you no longer need them, or you are experiencing unpleasant side-effects, or you are worried about becoming dependent on them.

On the other hand, you may be worried about what will happen if you do give them up – will you have nasty withdrawal symptoms; what if your Anxiety resurfaces once the medication is taken away?

Problems with medication have focused mainly on the group of tranquillisers known as benzodiazepines: diazepam (Valium), chlordiazepoxide (Librium), lorazepam (Ativan) and alprazolam (Xanax), as well as those used to help with sleep: temazepam, nitrazepam and flunitrazepam (Rohypnol). The main problems are that tolerance develops (which means that you need higher doses to achieve the same effect) and withdrawal symptoms occur if you try to come off these drugs too quickly.

More recently there has also been a lot of talk about whether anti-depressants, and particularly some of the newer classes of anti-depressants like Seroxat and Prozak, can cause similar problems.

The decision whether or not to continue taking the drugs is not always an easy one. You need to weigh up whether they are helping against the disadvantages.

Benzodiazepines can cause a range of side effects, the most common being confusion, stumbling, memory loss, drowsiness, light-headedness, a hangover effect (feeling the effects of the drug the next day), and an increase in aggression. They can impair your ability to drive or operate machinery, and can also be dangerous if mixed with alcohol. This can place restrictions on your ability to work, your freedom of movement and can interfere with enjoyment of social activities or pastimes which require mental alertness.

Current advice to doctors is to only prescribe these drugs for short periods (two to four weeks) and only for severe Anxiety. However, people who were prescribed these drugs before the dangers were fully recognised are still taking them because they are afraid to stop. It's important to come off these drugs slowly. Don't ever just stop taking them. This can cause unpleasant, and possibly dangerous, physical symptoms including convulsions.

The first step is to talk things over with your doctor. If on balance you feel you would be better off without the drugs, then ask him or her about helping you to withdraw from them. If your doctor is not experienced in tranquilliser withdrawal, then ask for a referral to someone who is.

The aim is to reduce your dosage very slowly, in small steps, with plenty of time to adjust to each reduction. This will reduce the risk of severe withdrawal symptoms and you will gradually start to feel more alert and energetic.

Many of the symptoms of withdrawal are similar to those of Anxiety and it may be difficult to tell whether what you are experiencing is temporary or whether the underlying Anxiety is resurfacing. Psychological support, either through self-help groups or from a professional therapist, can be helpful at this time to help you understand what is going on and also to learn new ways of coping without going back to the drugs.

4. More about anxiety disorders

Agoraphobia and claustrophobia

These are likely to include fears of some or all of the following:

1. Public places especially where there are many people, such as shopping centres or large gatherings. (The word itself derives from the Greek word 'agora' meaning market place.)

2. Being away from home, which represents safety. How far and how long varies, according to how severe your agoraphobia is. You may be unable to leave home at all, or you may be able to travel within a familiar circuit, knowing that you can return easily.

3. Travelling by public transport.

4. Travelling by car.

5. Crossing bridges.

6. Standing in a queue, e.g. at a supermarket checkout or in a bank.

7. Sitting at the dentist or hairdressers, in the cinema or theatre, or in a restaurant.

8. Being in an enclosed space such as a lift or tunnel.

Agoraphobia and claustrophobia may begin with a single incident of panic but become more generalised because of fear of losing control or fainting in any public situation from which it is difficult to escape.

You will need to set separate goals for each category, and construct an exposure ladder of steps towards each goal.

Specific phobias

There are many specific phobias, which can be put into groups. The authority most widely used by psychiatrists and other professionals worldwide is the Diagnostic and Statistical Manual 4th Edition 1994 (or DSM-IV) published in the United States and available online. This gives the following categories for the most common specific phobias:

- Animal type phobias, including insects and reptiles, bees, wasps, spiders, snakes, cats, dogs, mice, birds.

- Natural environment type (those involving physical situations or natural phenomena, e.g. heights, storms, earthquakes).

- Situational type like the fear of small confined spaces and being afraid of the dark.

- Blood/injection/injury type, like the fear of medical procedures including needles, hospitals.

- Other type (such as situations that might lead to illness, choking, vomiting).

If you have a particular phobia which you do not think is covered here, you may find it listed on The Phobia List website (see Appendix 2).

Remember, whatever it is called, and whatever the circumstances which trigger it, the root is always Anxiety, and the way to recovery is similar.

Some phobias might belong in one category or another, depending on what the actual trigger is, or be part of a more complex condition such as agoraphobia.

Social phobia (also called social anxiety disorder)

This is a complex condition, covering a range of fears to do with behaving or performing in front of other people. If you have social phobia you will worry about people looking at you and noticing what you are doing. You fear that you will do something which will be embarrassing or humiliating, or that people will be critical of you or reject you. You may be very self-conscious about your appearance or body size/shape, or have doubts about your ability to do or say the right thing.

Typical situations which cause anxiety are:

1. Attending social gatherings.

2. Eating or drinking in public.

3. Preparing food or drink or writing while being watched.

4. Taking part in physical activities such as swimming or going to the gym.

5. Using public lavatories.

6. Giving a public performance, speech or presentation.

7. Any kind of personal confrontation.

Some people are only anxious about one particular type of activity. Many people who are required to 'perform' as part of their profession – actors, musicians, teachers, politicians – suffer in this way before a public appearance. For others, it applies across most activities which involve being with other people.

The physical symptoms which accompany social phobia, such as blushing, sweating, trembling, palpitations, stammering and nausea cause additional distress to the sufferer and create a vicious circle. Blushing and emetophobia (the fear of being sick) in particular are often experienced as problems in their own right and there are specialised leaflets and advice available on these through the self-help organisations listed in Appendix 2.

Worrying about your behaviour, and what other people are thinking of you, can make it very difficult to be with other people. Your high anxiety makes it more likely that you will find yourself unable to say or do the things that you feel you should be doing, and more likely that you will continue to worry after the event that you have done or said something wrong.

Health anxiety

This is a condition which falls somewhere between phobia and obsession. It involves being preoccupied with fears of having a serious disease, or the idea that one has such a disease, based in misinterpretation of one's bodily sensations or changes. Behaviour associated with this includes:

- Repeatedly checking one's body.

- Reassurance seeking (e.g., from doctors or friends and family) that one does not have serious symptoms or diseases.

- Repeated requests for medical tests.

- Checking other sources of medical information (e.g., Internet searches of medical websites).

- Avoiding or escaping disease-related stimuli such as TV programmes or newspapers.

- Treating yourself as an invalid (e.g. avoiding any exertion in case it brings on a heart attack).

5. Other related disorders

Body dysmorphic disorder (BDD)

BDD is a disorder characterized by an excessive preoccupation with a real or imagined defect in physical appearance, such as such as a certain facial feature or imperfections of the skin. People with this disorder often think of themselves as ugly or disfigured, and have problems controlling negative thoughts about their appearance, even when reassured by others that they look fine and that the minor or perceived flaws aren't noticeable or excessive. They often have low self-esteem and fears of rejection from others.

Some sufferers realize that their perception of the 'defect' is distorted, but are unable to control the impulse to think about it. Others may adopt compulsive rituals to look at, hide, cover and/or improve their defect(s). They may spend a great deal of time looking at themselves in anything mirror-like and trying to convince others of how ugly they are. They may be compulsive in searching our doctors to treat them with medications and/or plastic surgery. Patients may go to any lengths to improve their appearance, including using methods that are dangerous.

BDD is not classified as an anxiety disorder. However, because of its similarities with some anxiety disorders (cf. social phobia, OCD and health anxiety) you may find the methods described in this book helpful. Some of the anxiety self-help organisations listed in Appendix 2 also offer advice on BDD. We would also recommend that you look for more specialised help through your doctor.

Eating disorders

This is another specialized group of disorders, primarily emotional in origin, but concerned with problems associated with food. The main types are:

● Anorexia Nervosa – where the person does not eat enough to maintain healthy body weight.

● Bulimia Nervosa – periods of overeating followed by vomiting or purging to control weight alternate with periods of starvation.

● Compulsive Overeating – binge eating – rapid consumption of large amounts of food in a short period of time.

Eating disorders develop through using food to cope with painful situations or feelings, or to relieve stress. There is considerable overlap between eating disorders and Anxiety disorders and many people may have both. If this is the case, you may find the methods suggested in this book useful, but as eating disorders are damaging to your physical health, and in severe cases life-threatening, we recommend that you also consult your doctor or contact an organisation specialising in eating disorders listed in the Appendix.

Chronic fatigue syndrome (Myalgic Encephalopathy or ME)

This illness is known by various names, these being the two most common names. Symptoms include:

● severe debilitating fatigue
● painful muscles and joints
● problems sleeping
● digestive problems
● poor memory
● poor concentration.

There is currently no agreement about whether this is a mental or physical health problem, and no universally accepted treatment, although rest during the acute phase and during any relapses seems to be crucial.

Chronic fatigue syndrome is not an Anxiety disorder, but sufferers who are well enough to follow the methods suggested in this book may find them useful.

Appendix 1
Professional help
including alternative and
complementary therapies

Cognitive behavioural therapy (CBT)

This is generally considered the most effective treatment for Anxiety disorders.

CBT is offered within the NHS by clinical psychologists or specially trained CBT therapists. This service is not as yet uniformly available throughout the country, and NHS waiting lists tend to be long. However, there are private CBT therapists and some counsellors and therapists from other approaches incorporate CBT techniques into their practice.

CBT principles are also used by community psychiatric nurses and voluntary agencies to support people with phobias carrying out exposure work. Other applications of CBT may be found in anxiety management or stress management courses.

Other therapies

We suggest you look at the guidelines published by the Royal College of Psychiatrists on using complementary therapies for mental health problems: www.rcpsych.ac.uk/mentalhealthinformation/therapies/complementarytherapy.aspx.

In Appendix 2 you will find contact details for the professional bodies that regulate some of the complementary and alternative therapies available, which may be helpful in treating anxiety disorders or relieving symptoms. It is important to choose a therapist who is well trained and regulated by a professional organisation.

Appendix 2
Directory

Self-help organisations

Anxiety UK (formerly National Phobics Society)

Zion Community Resource Centre

339 Stretford Road

Hulme

Manchester M15 4ZY

Tel: 08444 775 774

Email: info@phobics-society.org.uk

Website: wwww.phobics-society.org.uk

Services include: 1:1 therapies such as CBT, clinical hypnotherapy and counselling. Email support, online support and telephone helpline. Has another project 'destigmatize' which offers information on anxiety disorders in Hindi, Punjabi and Urdu

Website: www.destigmatize.org.uk.

First Steps to Freedom

PO Box 476

Newquay

Cornwall TR7 1WQ

Tel: 0845 120 2916 (helpline 10 am to 10 pm)

Tel: 0845 841 0619 (admin Line)

Email: first.steps@btconnect.com

Website: www.first-steps.org

Free confidential telephone helpline providing information and advice on strategies to help sufferers and carers deal with the symptoms of anxiety. Detailed guidance and on-going help and support to members. Individual mentoring. All volunteers are trained to the THA Quality Standard.

No Panic
93 Brands Farm Way
Telford TF3 2JQ
Tel: 0808 808 0545 Helpline (every day of the year 10 am to 10 pm)
Tel: 01952 590 005 (office, Monday–Friday, 9.30 am to 4.30 pm)
Email: ceo@nopanic.org.uk
Website www.nopanic.org.uk

Offers a national helpline and also provides a range of literature, audiocassettes and CDs, videocassettes, DVDs, and recovery groups, by telephone.

OCD Action
Davina House
Suites 506–507
137–149 Goswell Road
London EC1V 7ET
Tel: 0845 360 6232 (helpline)
Tel: 0870 360 6232 (office line)
Email: info@ocdaction.org.uk
Website: www.ocdaction.org.uk

Information and support to those suffering from obsessive-compulsive spectrum disorders including OCD, body dysmorphic disorder, trichotillomania, compulsive skin picking and hoarding.

OCD-UK
PO Box 8955
Nottingham
NG10 9AU
Website: www.ocduk.org

Independently working with and for people with obsessive compulsive disorder.

Triumph Over Phobia (TOP UK)
PO Box 3760
Bath
BA2 3WY
Tel: 0845 600 9601
Email: info@topuk.org
Website: www.topuk.org

Self-help therapy groups for sufferers of phobia, OCD and other related anxiety. Groups meet weekly and are supportive, warm and friendly. The charity also runs a helpline for information and advice.

General information on mental health and associated problems

The Royal College of Psychiatrists
17 Belgrave Square
London
SW1X 8PG
Tel: 020 7235 2351
Fax: 020 7245 1231
Email: rcpsych@rcpsych.ac.uk
Website: www.rcpsych.ac.uk

Produces a comprehensive range of literature on all aspects of mental health including alcohol and depression, prescribed drugs and books and leaflets for children and young people.

NHS Direct:
Tel: 0845 4647 24 (available 24 hours)
Website: www.nhsdirect.nhs.uk

BUPA
Website: www.bupa.co.uk

Mind
MindinfoLine
PO Box 277
Manchester
M60 3XN
Tel: 0845 766 0163
Email : info@mind.org.uk
Website: www.mind.org.uk

Works to create a better life for everyone with experience of mental distress. MindinfoLine provides information on a broad range of mental health topics including where to get help if you, or a friend or family member, are distressed.

Phobias

List of phobias:
The Phobia List
Website: www: phobialist.com

Dental phobias:
British Dental Health Foundation
Tel: 0870 333 1188 (Helpline)
Website: www.beyondfear.org

Flying phobias:
Flying without fear (Virgin Atlantic)
Tel: 01423 714900
Website: www.flyingwithoutfear.co.uk

Aviatours (British Airways)
Website: www.aviatours.co.uk

Professional help including alternative and complementary therapies

Counselling and psychotherapy

Cognitive behavioural therapy
British Association for Behavioural and Cognitive Psychotherapies (BABCP)
Victoria Buildings
9–13 Silver Street
Bury
BL9 0EU
Tel: 01254 875 277
Fax: 01254 239 114
Email: babcp@babcp.com
Website: www.babcp.com, then click 'find a therapist'

OCTC (the Oxford Cognitive Therapy Centre)
Psychology Dept
Warneford Hospital
Oxford
OX3 7JX
Tel: 01865 223986
Website: www.octc.co.uk

Self-help booklets on anxiety disorders.

General counselling/psychotherapy
British Association for Counselling and Psychotherapy (BACP)
BACP House
Unit 15
St John's Business Park
Lutterworth
Leicestershire
LE17 4HB
Tel: 0870 443 5219
Email: information@bacp.co.uk

Online directory of counsellors/psychotherapists, see: www.bacp.co.uk
select 'find a therapist' and then your location.

United Kingdom Council for Psychotherapy (UKCP)
2nd Floor
Edward House
2 Wakley Street
London
EC1V 7LT
Email: info@psychotherapy.org.uk

Online directory: www. psychotherapy.org.uk

United Kingdom Register of Counsellors and Psychotherapists
Address as for BACP.
Tel: 0870 443 5232

At the time of writing, there is no statutory regulation of counselling and psychotherapy, but within the next year or two these professions will have to be registered with the Health Professions Council. Once this comes into force, practitioners registered with the UKRC will transfer to the new register. For details of counsellors and psychotherapists currently registered see: www.bacp.co.uk, select 'UKRC'.

Relate

Tel: 0300 100 1234

Website: www.relate.org.uk

Relationship counselling and sex therapy. Also offers a range of other relationship support services.

Appendix 3
Book List

The Anxiety and Phobia Workbook by Edmund J. Bourne, Ph.D. New Harbinger Pubns Inc, 4th Rev Ed edition 2005, ISBN-10: 1572244135; ISBN-13: 978-1572244139. A very comprehensive guide to overcoming anxiety disorders which we recommend highly to readers seeking fuller information on the ideas and methods we have described. It contains a fuller description of the sub-personalities referred to in Part Three, which were first described by Dr R. Reid Wilson in his book *Don't Panic: taking control of Anxiety Attacks*.

Assertiveness: Step By Step by Windy Dryden and Daniel Constantinou. Sheldon Press, ISBN: 0-85969-925 0.

Beyond Fear by Dorothy Rowe. HarperCollins, Paperback, 2007, ISBN10: 0007246595; ISBN13: 9780007246595. One of many titles by this psychologist offering guidance and inspiration to those seeking happiness through self-knowledge.

Coping Successfully with Panic Attacks by Shirley Trickett. Sheldon Press, 1992, ISBN-10: 0859696464; ISBN-13: 978-0859696463.

Essential Help for your Nerves by Dr. Claire Weekes. Thorsons, 2000, ISBN-10: 0722540132; ISBN-13: 978-0722540138.

Feel the Fear and Do It Anyway: How to Turn Your Fear and Indecision into Confidence and Action by Susan Jeffers. Vermilion, Paperback, 20th Anniversary edition, 2007, ISBN-10: 0091907071; ISBN-13: 978-0091907075. Also available on Audio Cassette, Simon & Schuster Audio. A self-help classic.

Manage Your Mood: How to use Behavioural Activation techniques to overcome depression by David Veale and Rob Willson. Constable and Robinson, 2007, ISBN-10: 1845293142; ISBN-13 9781845293147.

Obsessive Compulsive Disorder: The facts by Padmal de Silva and Stanley Rachman. OUP, paperback, 2004, ISBN-10: 0198520824; ISBN-13: 978-0-19-852082-5.

Overcoming Social Anxiety and Shyness by Gillian Butler, Robinson, paperback, 1999, ISBN-10: 1854877038; ISBN-13: 978-1854877031.

When Once is Not Enough – Help for Obsessive Compulsives by Gail Steketee and Kerrin White. New Harbinger Publications, 1991. ISBN-10: 0934986878; ISBN-13: 978-0934986878.

A Woman in Your Own Right: Assertiveness and You by Anne Dickson. Quartet Books, 1982, ISBN-10: 0704334208; ISBN-13: 978-0704334205. A clear and straightforward guide to becoming more assertive which is helpful to both women and men.

Index

If you want to know how...

365 Steps to Self-Confidence

Learning to Counsel

365 Ways to be your Own Life Coach

Healing the Hurt Within

Acupuncture for Body, Mind and Spirit

howtobooks

Send for a free copy of the latest catalogue to:

How To Books

Spring Hill House, Spring Hill Road, Begbroke

Oxford OX5 1RX, United Kingdom.

info@howtobooks.co.uk

howtobooks.co.uk